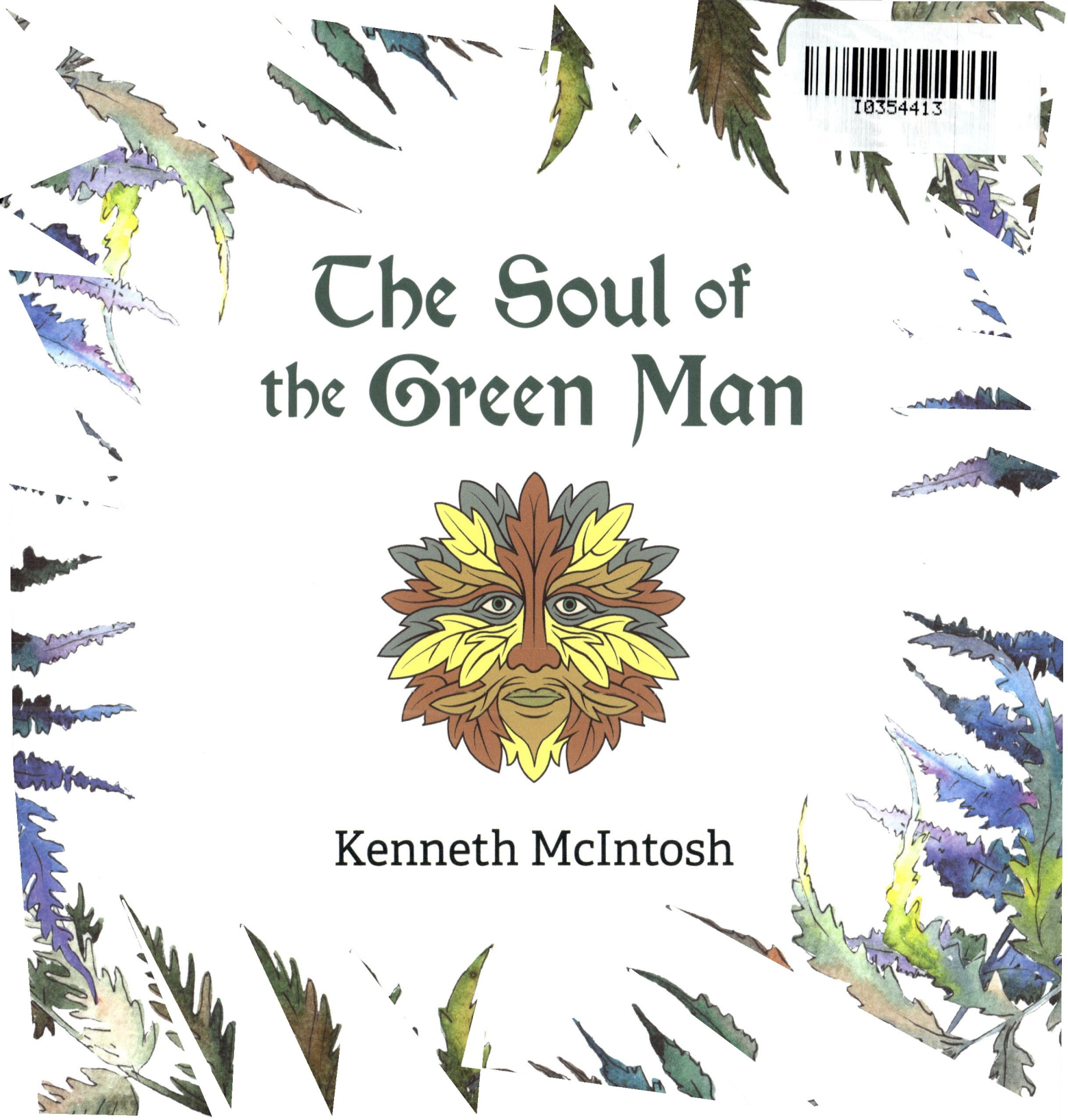

The Soul of the Green Man

Kenneth McIntosh

ANAMCHARA BOOKS

The world is so full of a number of things,

I'm sure we should all be as happy as kings.

—Robert Louis Stevenson

The Soul of the Green Man

Copyright © 2020 by Anamchara Books, a division of Harding House Publishing Service, Inc. All rights reserved. No part of this publication may be reproduced or transmitted in any form or by any means, electronic or mechanical, including photocopying, recording, taping, or any information storage and retrieval system, without permission from the publisher.

Scripture quotations labeled NIV are from the Holy Bible, New International Version®, NIV® Copyright © 1973, 1978, 1984, 2011 by Biblica, Inc.® Used by permission. All rights reserved worldwide. Scripture quotations labeled NRSV are from the New Revised Standard Version Bible, copyright © 1989 the Division of Christian Education of the National Council of the Churches of Christ in the United States of America. Used by permission. All rights reserved.

ANAMCHARA BOOKS
Vestal, New York 13850
www.anamcharabooks.com

Design and layout by Micaela Grace.

ISBN: 978-1-62524-502-1

Contents

Author's Note	9
1. Have You Seen the Jack in the Green?	13
2. Leafy Faces in Medieval Places	25
3. Green Man Hide-and-Seek	39
4. What About the Green *Women*?	51
5. The Green Man's Magical Medieval World	61
6. Lady Julia Introduces the Green Man to Society	79
7. The Family Tree	87
8. The Green Man in King Arthur's Court	101
9. Jack and the Maypole	113
10. The Green Man and His Merry Men	127
11. A Wise (Green) Man from the East	137
12. The Green Man at the Sacred Threshold	143
13. In the Temples of the Warrior Monks	155
14. All Flesh Is Grass	167
15. The Myth Behind the Face	175
16. The Perennial Green Man	185

Author's Note

This is a story that involves many journeys—and no one travels completely alone. This book would not be possible were it not for the assistance of church volunteers and staff (guides, vergers, wardens, and rectors) whose names I regrettably neglected to write down. I wonder if they thought, "Not another tourist wanting to see the Green Man," but they acted cheerful and half the time I wouldn't have found him without their service.

This private obsession would not have then been shared with the public without a little more help from my friends. David Cole has added much to my journeys in

England sharing his friendship, knowledge, and ideas. Other members of the Community of Aidan and Hilda in the UK have also helped my journeying. Jude McKenzie and Todd Barnell, both officers of the Northern Arizona Celtic Heritage Society, encouraged me to give a talk on the Green Man for the Flagstaff Highland Festival. Martha Shideler subsequently asked me to convert that talk into written form and published the resulting three-part article in issues of the *Independent Celt Newsletter.*

The original presentations first made their way into e-book form with the alchemical magic of Ellyn Sanna at Anamchara Books. She grew the original short article into first a short Kindle book, and now she has helped me to create an expanded print-format book, improving it at every stage. More than that, her presence and friendship added much joy to visits at UK sites in this book.

Inspired by the Green Man found in a choir stall in the twelfth- to thirteenth-century cathedral in Poitiers, France. The leaves that surround his face are probably acanthus (though they might also be oak).

Finally, my life companion Marsha makes all my travels delightful. I keep wondering if she is ever going to say, "Oh no, not another old church," but she has repeatedly risked becoming lost in the English countryside looking for obscure chapels, has fought for parking spaces near cathedrals in the cities, and peered into the corners with me to find the wonders of each medieval space.

With such companions in life, I am a wealthy man.

The Green Man is moving from the realms of dusty antiquarian pursuits into popular culture. There are more Green Man books published, websites, and Facebook sites. With so much information available, this book cannot claim to be definitive in knowledge or scope, yet I am hopeful that my experiences and musings may prove helpful even to those who are already well acquainted with the Green Man.

I invite you to come with me on my journeys as I came to know the soul of the Green Man.

—***Kenneth McIntosh***

The original inspiration for this image is found under a thirteenth-century choir seat in Worcester Cathedral.

1

Have You Seen the Jack in the Green?

"Have you seen the Jack in the Green?" asked the English Rock Band Jethro Tull in their 1977 album *Songs from the Wood*.

Yes, I have.

I have seen him in his better-known guise, the Green Man, carved in stone in medieval chapels and cathedrals. He danced beside me in a crowded street during an English May Fair and moved to the pulsing beat at a rave in Salt Lake City. He pops out at me from the pages of novels, and he's thrilled me on the theater screen. Yet I was almost fifty years old before I first sighted him.

A decade ago, my wife and I were on pilgrimage in what I call "my city" in Ireland. Like me, Kilkenny is named after Saint Kenneth (or Canice in Old Irish). A bust of Saint Canice stands in the city square, Saint Canice's holy well still gushes out water, and the massive Cathedral Church of St. Canice stands as an enduring monument to his memory.

St. Canice's Cathedral in Kilkenny was built in the thirteenth century, but the round tower that stands beside it dates from the ninth century. An earlier wooden church stood on the same location, which has been the site of Christian worship since the sixth century.

I was like a kid in a candy store as a guide led us through the stone edifice, pointing out its peculiar delights. "And up there," she gestured upward with a flourish, "is our Green Man."

A young man's face, carved from stone, protruded from one of the arches high above us; he looked like he was singing happily, perhaps a member of the cathedral's medieval choir, mouth wide open belting out notes. But those weren't musical notes coming out of his mouth. They were leaves.

This is the stone face in St. Canice Cathedral that first drew me into my ongoing fascination with the Green Man.

As our guide explained the history of the Green Man to us (incorrectly, as I learned much later), we listened in fascination. Shortly after that, in another medieval church, we spotted another Green Man. And thus began our search for his foliated visage in numerous medieval churches throughout the British Isles.

Later, I learned about Jack in the Green, the Green Man's persona in folk dances and pageants of the Isles. That transformed him from a static work of art, bound by ancient confines of wood and stone, to a moving reality in today's world. I realized he had stepped out from the long-ago past and become a twenty-first-century cultural influence.

The gaze of a modern-day stained-glass Green Man challenges us to learn his secret.

In whatever form he takes, whenever I see a Green Man, I'm drawn by his eyes. As the cliché puts it, eyes are windows into the soul, and I can't help but wonder: *What secrets lie hidden in the Green Man's soul?* His face is sometimes hard to read, obscured by acanthus leaves or painted dark green. Yet the eyes jump out from behind this leafy concealment, alert and wise. The stone faces are mute, and Jack in the Green dancing among the mummers does not sing. But the eyes say, *I have a hidden meaning. I was portrayed in a thousand different ways in the past, and I keep sprouting again and again down through the centuries. Don't you want to know who I am?*

The Green Man's core identity is indeed hidden, for in all the writing that survives from the Middle Ages, not a single document says, "You know those faces with the leaves that we carved in hundreds of churches? Well, those represent such-and-such." A notebook from 1230 by French artist Villard de Honnecourt does contain several faces that we would now call Green Men. The artist labeled his drawings simply "faces with leaves"—and told us nothing of the meaning of those faces or what they represented.

Reproduction of the sketches from the notebook of Villard de Honnecourt. Villard's notebook is filled with architectural details, so his drawings of "faces with leaves" were likely details from stonework he had seen. Most scholars today believe his notebook likely served as a pattern book containing designs for manuscript illumination or metalwork.

Other medieval images can be interpreted because the tales that convey their meaning have been preserved over the centuries. Portrayals of Bible stories, the saints, the Virgin Mary, and other religious portrayals are still symbols used in Christianity. Various occupation such as the baker, the blacksmith, the priest, and the fisherman can be readily identified. Mythological creatures such as dragons, mermaids, and unicorns correspond with stories preserved from medieval times until now. But where are stories that explain the leaf-sprouting face of the Green Man?

And he is clearly symbolic. All those Green Men didn't appear because one stone mason said, "I think I'll chisel some leaves coming out of this bloke's mouth," and then the design just caught on and became the rage. No, the Green Man has an instantly recognizable and strong sense of identity. He represented something important to medieval people.

As a symbol, even today, the Green Man is multivalent, and the same would have been true in the Middle Ages, when his face first became so popular. His image can be found across Europe—so even if we could know what an artist carving a Green Man in Giles Cathedral, in Edinburgh, Scotland, understood that image to mean, that could very well mean something quite different for, say, another mason carving a Green Man at the same time in Santiago, Spain. Furthermore, symbols are always being reinterpreted. That is part of the Green Man's continuing fascination.

For an example of how a single Green Man can produce a variety of interpretations, consider this drawing of a Green Man with grapes. There are similar depictions in multiple locations, both ancient and modern. The grapevine growing from his mouth has a long and rich symbolism, leading to a variety of possible conjectures about this image.

This drawing is based on a fifteenth-century carving in Dunblane Cathedral in Scotland.

The Classical world connected grapevines with the god Dionysus (the Romans called him Bacchus), who was associated with rebirth after death. His return to life after being dismembered was symbolically represented by the grapevines, which must be pruned back sharply and become dormant in winter for them to bear fruit the following year.

Christianity has often been at pains to separate Christ from any parallels with Pagan gods, but Jesus himself may have been aware of the connection to the Greek god when he said, "I am the vine" (John 15:5) and compared the Realm of Heaven to a vineyard (Matthew 20:1). By claiming the symbolism of grapes for himself, Jesus connected himself not only to the Hebrew scriptures (where Israel is compared to a vine) but also to the Greek and Roman cultures that dominated his day.

This ancient Roman statue portrays Bacchus with his head surrounded by grapes and grape leaves. He (and his Greek counterpart, Dionysus) was considered to be important to everyday life because of his ability to actively influence and empower his followers.

This reproduction of a medieval drawing portrays Jesus with a grapevine growing out from the wound in his side, graphically illustrating the concept that Jesus' death brings growing green life and burgeoning fruitfulness.

Have You Seen the Jack in the Green?

Jesus was in some sense a Green Man, bringing new life to both the spiritual and natural world.

So we have rich and edifying symbolism. But wait! A church historian looks at these Green-Man-with-grapes portrayals and sees a moral warning. Medieval images often show the grapes coming out of his mouth, indicating that perhaps the Green Man had too much to drink and he's vomiting grapes. It's a warning against intoxication.

Green Man from Southwell Minster, created around 1100.

Is this Green Man a remembrance of ancient Bacchus, a symbol of Christ, or a plea for sobriety? Experts in art and history disagree. And that's a good thing to remember as you peruse this book. I'll quote people with ideas about the Green Man, and I'll tell you what I think of some interpretations. But who really knows? And that's part of the fascination of the Green Man, and why he's so much fun. In the end, you get to choose what the Green Man means for you.

From a Green Man in Wells Cathedral in Somerset, England.

This book is an invitation to journey with me through the British Isles, staring into the Green Man's eyes. The tone is more whimsical than academic, because my Green Man travels have been largely serendipitous. I've looked for him wherever I happen to be, and then I've tried to learn more from research each time I see him.

I don't promise to reveal all the Green Man's mysteries; Jack likes to hide in the Green, concealing his nature. But those piercing eyes invite us to look behind the leafy mask. They promise both meaning and mystery. So come, let's search for the soul of the Green Man.

Based on a carving found in Sussex, England, this Green Man has acanthus leaves sprouting from his face. This is the most common plant to be found in medieval Green Men.

Leafy Faces in Medieval Spaces

During the Middle Ages, Green Men were created as architectural ornaments, especially in churches. They show up in more than two hundred churches in the British Isles, and there are more than a thousand examples. Art scholars refer to him as a "foliated head"—a face with obvious human features (eyes, nose, and mouth) and vegetation growing out from at least one orifice (most often the mouth but sometimes the nose, and less commonly the eyes and ears).

Because the Green Man is common to Celtic regions, he's sometimes assumed to be a Celtic symbol. However, he also appears in medieval churches and cathedrals throughout Europe, and variations on the Green Man theme can be found globally. My own travels and research have been in England, Ireland, Scotland, and Wales, so that is the primary scope of this book, but travelers in other parts of the world will have their own encounters with our leafy friend.

It can be a bit tricky trying to decide, "Is this a Green Man or not?" For example, laurel crowns may appear to be hair, or eyebrows in a carving may seem leaf-like. Solar beams or a lion's mane that surround a male bearded face can seem like foliage. I don't count such images as a Green Men, though. My rule is that when clearly identifiable leafy matter is coming right out of his face—that's a Green Man.

These faces could be mistaken for Green Men—but they're not. The face on the left does have leaves on his head—but they are laurel leaves, indicating that this man (a fifth-century worshipper at Apollo's sanctuary on Cyprus) was crowned with victory and eternal glory. The middle face is surrounded by solar rays, not leaves. And the face on the right (from a bronze drinking horn) portrays a man with a lion's mane.

The foliage can be any kind of leaves, including ferns, plant leaves, or leaves from various species of trees—but acanthus leaves are the most common foliage seen on Green Men. These are often mistaken for oak leaves, a mistake I made myself until just recently. For centuries, however, the acanthus plant has been associated with life that endures beyond the grave. It was a common element in Greek cemetery carvings since before the time of Christ, and it has remained a popular decorative motif throughout Europe and North America. Its connection with Green Man images indicates the connection this archetypal symbol has with the power of life to overcome death.

From left to right: a living acanthus leaf; stylized acanthus leaves on a column of the Temple of Artemis in Ephesus, dating from the fourth century before the Common Era; a relatively modern-day gravestone with acanthus leaves.

Leafy Faces in Medieval Spaces

Although acanthus leaves are by far the most common Green Man foliage, these Green Men show the range of plant species that can be seen emerging from their faces. From left to right, top: a fifteenth-century German Green Man has ivy trailing from his lips; a fourteenth-century Green Man from the ceiling of Norwich Cathedral spews out staghorn ferns; wild geranium leaves and blossoms grow from the mouth and scalp of a thirteenth-century Green Man on the exterior of the Southwell Minster chapterhouse in Nottinghamshire. From left to right, bottom: from the ceiling of Exeter Cathedral, these Green Men have a riot of wild carrot leaves spraying out from their throats; a drawing based on another Green Man from the Southwell Minster chapterhouse, this one has cinquefoil leaves and blossoms branching from his mouth; a French medieval Green Man carved beneath a choir seat has oak leaves and acorns issuing from his eyes and mouth.

The Green Man first appears in the British Isles around the time of the Norman Invasion, in the latter part of the eleventh century. This is a time when the Normans were seeking to recapture the glory of ancient Roman art, resulting in the Romanesque style of European architecture. Green Men made in this era do not represent distinct human faces. I found a good example of a particularly ancient Romanesque Green Man at Brecon Cathedral in Powys, Wales.

In 2016, my wife Marsha and I had spent a delightful day driving through the remote lush green hills of the Brecons. Come evening, we had worked up an appetite, and Brecon was the closest town large enough to offer a restaurant. We drove into town past the cathedral; when we decided to stop and investigate, we found that evensong was about to begin. (If you've never heard a Welsh choir and you ever take a trip to Wales, enjoy all the singing you can!) After the service, we shook hands with the clergy who happened to be standing beside a very large and ancient-looking baptismal font that—*aha!*—had four Green Men carved around its circumference, interleaved with symbols of the Gospels. I mentioned it, and one of the priests smiled.

"Ah yes, the Old Green Man," he said and proceeded to say that for a thousand years the children of the community have been christened with water from that vessel.

The cathedral's website states that the font dates from "1150 (but perhaps two hundred years before that)." If it does in fact date to 950, it is the earliest carved Green Man in a church in the Isles, but apparently its exact date cannot be proved.

Look at the face of a Green Man on that baptismal font and you'll see it is not a portrait of any particular individual; in fact, I can't tell if the face is that of a man or a beast. The leaves are highly stylized as well, matching the lovely

Celtic knotwork above it, resembling art in the borders of manuscripts from the Early Middle Ages, such as the famous Book of Kells.

Green Men proliferate during the Gothic era of church architecture, between 1200 and the beginning of the Reformation in the sixteenth century. During this era, they become more three dimensional, the foliage carving becomes more naturalistic, and the faces are portraits of real people.

We spent a week in Devon in 2016 and had a day to explore, so we stopped at Ottery St. Mary Church. The whole building is exquisite, founded in 1337 for a college of monks. Samuel Taylor Coleridge, one of the great artistic and philosophical influences of the nineteenth century, grew up worshiping at this church. As we walked between the pews, our heads tilted back, we had a sense of openness and light, and we experienced a time of prayer and refreshment there.

If you look at the Green Men on the pillars of Ottery

Babies are still baptized in the ancient font in Brecon Cathedral. Note the fantastical creatures enclosed within the vines.

The Soul of the Green Man

These two Green Gentleman on pillars at the Parish Church of Ottery St. Mary, Devon, England, portray actual individuals. Comparing these Green Men with that in Brecon Cathedral gives you a sense of the differences between Green Men carved before and after the Gothic period.

St. Mary's church, you are immediately struck by the realistic nature of their depiction. You can imagine what it would be like to meet them in person. One of the gentleman has his eyes closed, but the other one stares out from wide eyes beneath heavy brows. As I looked up at him, I felt like saying "Hey, what are you doing stuck up there?" I sensed an urgency in his stare, as if he were saying, *Come closer. I have important things to tell you.* (In fact, the Green Men at St. Mary Ottery Church did

Leafy Faces in Medieval Spaces   **31**

impart an important clue as to the Green Man's medieval identity, but I'll speak of that later in this book.)

Over the years, as we traveled around the UK, we learned that we might find a Green Man on either the interior or the exterior of a church. Most often he is carved out of stone, but he can also appear in the woodwork. Sometimes he is carved on the bottom of a misericord—a shelf-like seat found in medieval choir stalls.

This thirteenth-century misericord in Worcester Cathedral portrays two Green Men on either side of a woman riding a goat. A misericord—sometimes called a "mercy seat"—was basically a ledge projecting from the underside of a hinged seat in a choir stall which, when the seat was turned up, gave support to someone standing. It allowed tired monastics the chance to take the weight off their feet.

This misericord shown to the left, from Worcester Cathedral, links the Green Man with women's cleverness and strength. The story it portrays is an ancient folktale, "The Wise Daughter," which was recorded by the Brothers Grimm in Germany but is also known in England and in Norse countries; the story was even used in an episode of the TV series *Vikings*.

The tale goes like this: A peasant received some land as a gift from the king. When the peasant and his daughter plowed the field, they found a mortar and pestle made of gold. The daughter warned that if they gave the mortar to the king in return for his generosity, he would ask for the pestle as well; the father, however, gave the mortar to the king anyway, and just as the daughter had predicted, the king demanded the pestle and put the father in prison until he got it. When the king heard the father loudly lamenting the fact that he hadn't listened to his daughter's wise advice, the king summoned the daughter and gave her a challenge: to come to him neither naked nor clothed, neither walking nor riding a horse, neither on the road nor off it, with a gift that cannot be received. If she could prove her cleverness, he would marry her, and her father would be released.

The carving between the Green Men on the Worcester misericord shows the daughter's solution: she is wrapped in a fishing net, riding a goat with one foot on the ground, and holding a hare—she is clothed but not clothed, not walking but not riding a horse, and carrying a gift that cannot be received (since it would hop away). Perhaps the artist who carved these images connected the Wise Daughter with the Green Man because both are tricksters (one masculine, one feminine), archetypal

Leafy Faces in Medieval Spaces

characters that theologian Peter Rollins defines as "revolutionary figures that challenge the natural order. They poke holes in what everyone takes for granted and fight systems that oppress." Rollins points out that Jesus was also a trickster.

Green Men can also be found carved on the ends of wooden pews, many of which are in southern England, in Somerset and Cornwall. In 2014, when I walked into St. Nonna's Church in Altarnun, Cornwall, I wasn't expecting Green Men; I had heard merely that St. Nonna's was "a quaint old church." As we stepped through the doorway, My wife Marsha was immediately attracted to a display concerning the wedding scene for the *Doc Martin* TV show that had been filmed at the church—but our friend Ellyn and I were awed by the pew ends. There were seventy-nine of them, carved gloriously in bas relief, dating to just before the Reformation.

Pew #48 is described in the church's guide book as "Green Man above chalice guarded by dragons or perhaps a merman with sea serpents?" This is a fascinating image on multiple levels. The multivalent nature of symbols is on display, insofar as the historian writing up the guidebook wasn't sure if the image portrays a

The author Ken McIntosh and Anamchara Books editor Ellyn Sanna study one of the pew ends at St. Nonna's church.

merman or a Green Man, dragons or sea serpents. The fact that this man, whatever he is, is coming out of a chalice—in a church—is fascinating, since there are numerous medieval portrayals like this portraying Christ emerging from a chalice. Theologians in this Gothic era emphasized the "real presence" of Christ transmitted via the communion cup, which means that this audacious image points to the Green Man as a Christ image. The "Cosmic Christ" in the New Testament was understood as "the soul of Nature," and the Green Man can likewise be understood as the intelligence or soul hidden within the natural world. Like Christ, the Green Man connects the realms of humankind and Nature. But what are those dragons/sea serpents doing drinking from the cup of Christ? Some images contain symbolism too deep to fathom. What I wouldn't give

The pew end in St. Nonna's Church portraying a Green Man/merman emerging from a chalice. Symbolically, a Green Man and a merman were not so very different; one pointed to the vital Spirit within Nature on land, while the other pointed to something very similar within the sea.

Leafy Faces in Medieval Spaces

to go back in time and speak with the artist who carved this bench end!

Curiously, there are other bench ends in a Somerset church that share some themes with the Altarnun Green Man. One of these sixteenth-century carvings in the Church of the Holy Ghost in Crowcombe, Somerset, has mermen shooting out from the Green Man's ears and grapevines from his mouth, while another one shows a two-tailed merman with foliage bursting from his lips and sea serpents from his ears. These Green Man images contain alchemical symbolism pointing toward the union of dualism: earth and water, body and soul, male and female. According to the alche-

This drawing is taken from one of the Green-Men-plus-merman pew ends in the Church of the Holy Ghost in Crowcombe, Somerset.

mists, the mermaid (or siren) connects to the "Universal Mercury"—the all-pervading World Soul that calls out to us through Nature and all things. Combining the Green Man with mermaids created a further union of forest and sea, the entire natural world.

Oh-so many Green Men! And each one points to a mystery, a wild and lovely strangeness at the heart of our world. If we have often forgotten and overlooked the Green Man's message to us, perhaps we can be forgiven—given the fact that the Green Man has sometimes chosen to hide himself, as we'll see in the next chapter.

Taken from a pew carving in Winchester Cathedral. Note the protruding tongue.

Green Man Hide-and-Seek

Where in churches will you find a Green Man? You never really know. I've seen it alleged that the Green Man was placed in hidden places, as though he were an embarrassment. And it is true that sometimes he can be hard to spot. I suspect, however, that the Green Man hides out of sheer mischief rather than any sense of shame.

Before we visited Wells Cathedral in 2015, our friend David Cole (the author of several Anamchara books) had told me that a fine specimen of the Green Man was there—but I couldn't find it. I walked most of the day in the cathedral, just soaking in the grandeur and aesthetic perfection of the place, but I had no luck finding that foliated head.

Wells Cathedral in Somerset is an imposing edifice.

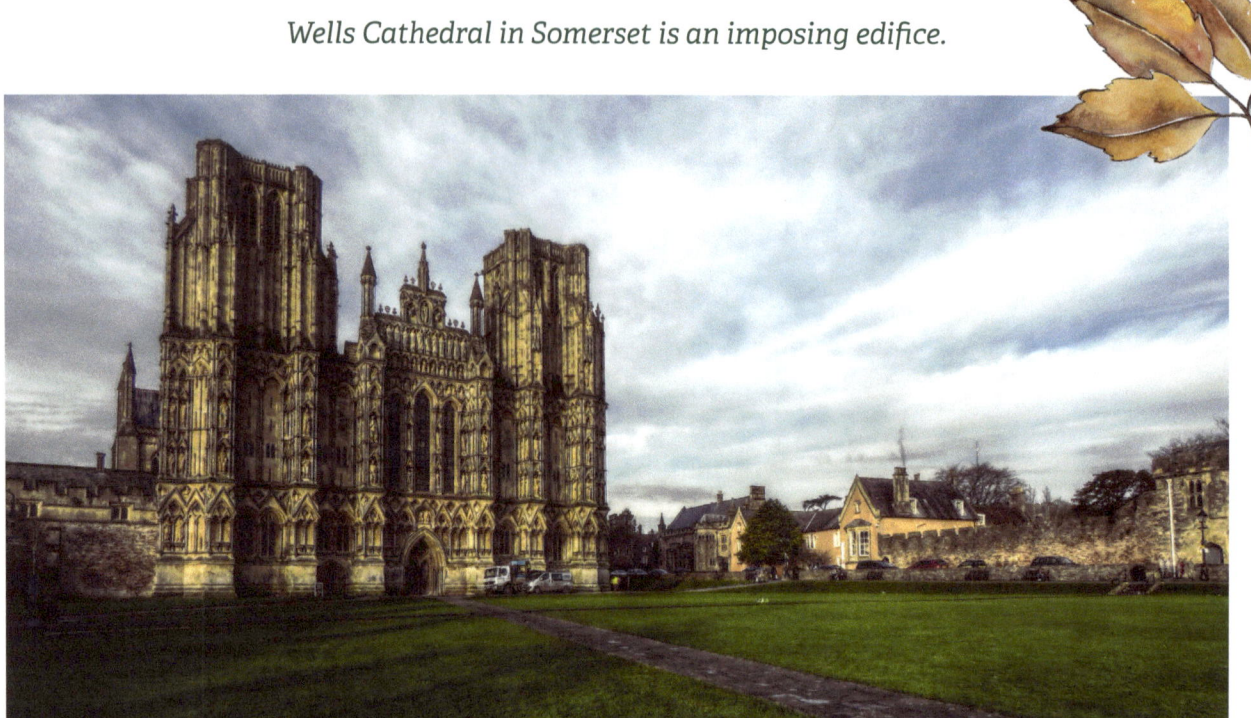

That evening, I texted David. As it turns out, there are quite a few Green Men hidden here and there in Wells Cathedral, but the one David had in mind is not on public view; I would have to ask to see it at the front desk of the cathedral. I was happy to return to the cathedral, where we spent another half day, and this time I did inquire at the visitors' entrance, where a volunteer directed me to track down the verger.

When I found the verger, he had an enormous iron keychain full of skeleton keys. He motioned me to follow, and we walked to an ancient-looking wooden door in the wall of the cathedral. That door was thick, rough-surfaced, and covered with dark-

The interior of Wells Cathedral is so vast that it's rather like wandering in an immense stone forest. No wonder that Green Men find plenty of hiding places there!

ened iron, like something out of a Harry Potter movie. After turning one of the skeleton keys in the lock, he pulled the door open on squeaky hinges, revealing a musty crypt in the wall. The verger pointed upward, and there—above the portal itself—was a detailed and puckish looking Green Man. He was hiding, but I didn't detect a trace of embarrassment in his expression.

Green Men also often hide their faces beneath misericords. As I mentioned in the previous chapter, misericords—or "mercy seats"—are shelf-like seats designed to aid tired members of a medieval choir by making it appear as though they were standing when in fact they had sat down to rest throughout the long service. Often times, images are carved on the bottom of the seat.

St. David's Cathedral is an ancient holy site with a long and tumultuous history. The original monastic community there was founded by Saint David, who died in 589. Between 645 and 1097, the community was attacked many times by Viking raiders, and many of its bishops were murdered by raiders and marauders. The present cathedral was begun in 1181 and completed not long after, but problems beset the new building, with the collapse of the new tower in 1220 and earthquake damage in 1247. Today, the building stands with an air of hard-won serenity.

In order to see the beauty hidden beneath the misericords, you must flip them up. Understandably, some churches are reluctant to have five-hundred-year-old bits of wood going up and down repeatedly on their aging hinges, so they are often unavailable for viewing. Some places of worship now display photos of the misericords so people can see their likenesses, while the actual carvings are preserved. But I have been lucky enough to see some of these.

You recall my enthusiasm for Welsh choirs; well, the singers are exceptional at St. David's Cathedral. The cathedral itself is impressive; its immensity dwarfs the tiny city around it. Inside one can walk and walk, through chambers that ooze history from the time of its founding Celtic saint through the Norman era and then the Gothic. The "new" ceiling was put up in the late Middle Ages.

And perhaps best of all, after an inspiring evensong choir service at St. David's Cathedral, a warden offered to flip up the misericords in the choir stalls so Marsha and I could see the carvings underneath. The misericords were each carved from a single piece of oak in the late fifteenth century. One of them was a powerful-looking Green Man.

The muscular, grimacing face on a misericord in St. David's Cathedral is slightly reminiscent of the very ancient Green Men on the Brecon Cathedral baptistry in the previous chapter, though this visage is obviously more human and realistic.

Both the Wells Cathedral Green Man and the St. David's misericord carving are examples of why I appreciate the kindness and assistance of church staff, both paid and volunteer. Shy Green Men might not come out of hiding without the help of these men and women. But on a trip in 2014, I found the elusive Green Men at Hereford Cathedral all on my own.

As I exited the cathedral along the newly restored St. John's Walk, a passage that dates to the twelfth century and is a covered walkway between the main cathedral and the cloisters, I happened to glance upward—and spied the carvings up in the beams that support the roof. I believe these were designed to be somewhat hidden, despite the effort that went into them. They cover a range of symbolic and mythical subjects, and one beam portrays a naked nun. (I wonder if she was a reminder to the priests that they must stay vigilant in avoidance of lust? The famous saint Thomas de Cantelupe, enshrined in the cathedral, must have walked this corridor, and one of the evidences given for his sainthood is that he never kissed a woman, not even his own sister.) To my great excitement, on the first wooden beam of St. John's Walk, after exiting the cathedral proper, I spotted a Green Man in all his leafy glory. St. John's Walk contains another Green Man, who was originally on a

Like the Green Men I saw in other locations in Wales, this one in Hereford's Cathedral also has a broad warrior's face, with a grimacing mouth and clenched teeth.

This drawing is based on the Green Man from Hereford Cathedral, who must have been a reminder to the holy men of the church: "Don't be all vinegar-faced. Lighten up, guys!" The protruding tongue shows the Green Man's cheeky and irreverent trickster side.

roof boss in the cathedral but fell from his perch long ago. Unlike many of his brothers, this little guy doesn't look angry or fearsome at all. In fact, of all the Green Men that I have seen, he wins the funny-face award.

The fact that many Green Men are sticking out their tongues has a variety of interpretations. Some authors say it shows the Green Man's wildness—or his sexuality and fertility. Other interpretations connect the gesture to what would have been the proper way to receive the Communion wafer. Perhaps it alludes to a verse in the Hebrew scriptures, Proverbs 15:4, which states, "A tongue that heals is a tree of life." Take your pick from all these meanings; there's room for them all!

In this chapter, I've been talking about the shy and elusive Green Man. Some writers in the past claimed that Green Men were typically placed in hard-to-see locations, covert symbols of unauthorized beliefs. From what you've read in this chapter, you might be nodding in agreement. Indeed, some Green Men seem to have been deliberately hidden—*but these wallflower Green Men are the exception rather than the rule.*

After a decade of looking for him, I'd say the Green Man prefers to be bold and in your face rather than tucked away. I'll explain his boldness more in another chapter; for now, I offer just one example of how "out there" the Green Man can be.

In 2015, Marsha and I were traveling in Scotland with extended family and stayed at Dornoch Castle, which is right across the street from the cathedral. After dark, I stepped out for some fresh air, decided to stroll over toward the cathedral, and there was the Green Man. I'd have had to be blind to miss him! I spied him immediately, even in the darkness. He is on the exterior of the cathedral, on the right side of the massive front entrance, at eye level.

The Green Man who greeted me outside Dornoch Cathedral.

You know how churches have greeters out in front, ensuring that no one makes it into the sanctuary without a smile, a handshake, and a bulletin? Dornoch is one of a half-dozen churches where I refer to the Green Man as a "church greeter," because he's in the obvious position to meet anyone heading into the building.

But this Green Man isn't the friendliest of greeters. His pouchy eyes, flared nose, clenched teeth, and tusk-like vines coming out of his mouth make him look as threatening as a wild boar. This was also the decided impression of the other members of my party when they saw him the next day.

In cases like this, when the Green Man looks more frightening than friendly, I think he serves a clearly *apotropaic* purpose. In the ancient world, apotropaic magic was intended to turn away harm or evil influences, and this Green Man is a guardian, keeping something or someone out. Nowadays, churches are desperate for worshipers and will practically pay people to walk in their doors, but in the Middle Ages, churches were more concerned with keeping sin, pestilence, and evil spirits outside their sanctuaries. Fearsome Green Men may have been like the gargoyles who were also considered to be a means of warding off evil.

Based on a ceiling boss in Crowland Abbey in Lincolnshire, England.

Or maybe this Green Man was intended as a warning to more tangible enemies? Bishop Gilbert de Moravia built Dornoch Cathedral in 1222. His predecessors had presided over their flock from Halkirk, but due to their brutal murder there, Gilbert chose to build Dornoch Cathedral at his own expense

Green Man Hide-and-Seek

This Green Man's original is found under a thirteenth-century misericord.

and moved the seat of his episcopacy to this safer location. The cathedral does look rather like a fortress. The Scottish church later recognized Gilbert as one of the noblest and wisest of their medieval leaders, and he was the last Scotsman given a place in the Calendar of Saints. Although we can't say for sure when the Dornoch Green Man was added to the cathedral, since the building has been damaged and rebuilt over the years, it's tempting to think that Bishop Gilbert could have placed that visage by the door as a stern warning to his human enemies.

Like Bishop Gilbert, the prelates of the medieval church were all male, and this relates to a commonly asked question: Why were there so many portrayals of Green *Men*? What about the women? Yes, clerics were male, but there are numerous medieval depictions of nuns, noble ladies, and peasant women. Medieval artists enjoyed portraying women. So why do we see—almost without exception—Green Men?

Well, that brings us to the next set of stops on our journey.

A modern portrayal of a Green Woman.

What About the Green Women?

I've spoken in a variety of venues about the Green Man: at Celtic festivals, churches, and in a pub. Whatever the venue, someone in the audience wants to know right out the gate, "What about a Green *Woman*?"

Today when women are making gains against harassment and stereotypes, and record numbers of women are achieving representation in governments worldwide, the absence of Green Women seems especially jarring. Is the Green Man a gendered idea, spawned by the patriarchy?

Feminine foliated heads in medieval churches are exceedingly rare, if they exist at all. I was excited, therefore, to encounter one in the Parish Church of St. Michael Archangel in Lyme Regis, Dorset, on a trip in 2014.

Marsha and I had gone to Lyme Regis because it was the home of Mary Anning, who is one of our heroes. A hundred years before any woman was allowed into the British Geologic Society, Mary unearthed fossils from the cliffs of Devon's Jurassic Coast. She discovered the ichthyosaurus and pterodactyl, and at a time when scientist didn't believe that any lifeforms had gone extinct on our planet (since the world was believed to be only 5,000 years old), Mary proved to a skeptical public that these prehistoric giants had come and gone from the Earth's stage a very long time ago. Self-taught, and poor her whole life, Mary Anning blazed a trail ahead of her male contemporaries in the Victorian scientific world. And she was a faithful member of the Lyme Regis Anglican church of St. Michael the Archangel, seeing no conflict between her scientific discoveries and her faith. There is a window and display honoring her in

I do have a lovely Green Woman in the foyer of my home, a gift from my sister. This Green Woman gazes across a doorframe at her masculine counterpart. They are both there to greet me each time I arrive home, balancing masculine and feminine energies. But this Green Woman is a recent artistic creation; there was no medieval image to use as a model for her face.

This drawing is based on the Green Woman in the church at Lyme Regis, where her face adorns the organ.

the nave of the church. So it seems fitting for Mary Anning's church to also have a Green Woman.

Initially, I was thrilled to discover this Green Woman, and in a church that is very old, dating back to the Saxon era. But after undergoing considerable effort to photograph this Green Lady, I discovered that she's rather young—in fact, created by

What About the Green Women?

a local artist in 2009. It's a nice addition to the Lyme Regis church, but I still had not seen a Green Woman from the Middle Ages.

More recently, I got excited again, thinking I'd found a genuine medieval Green Woman. I was in *ooh-aah!* mode in the Chapter House of Southwell Minster, which had been on my travel bucket list for some time. We finally made it there in 2018, and I was not disappointed. It's as grand as any cathedral, and the treasure of Southwell Minister is its Chapter House.

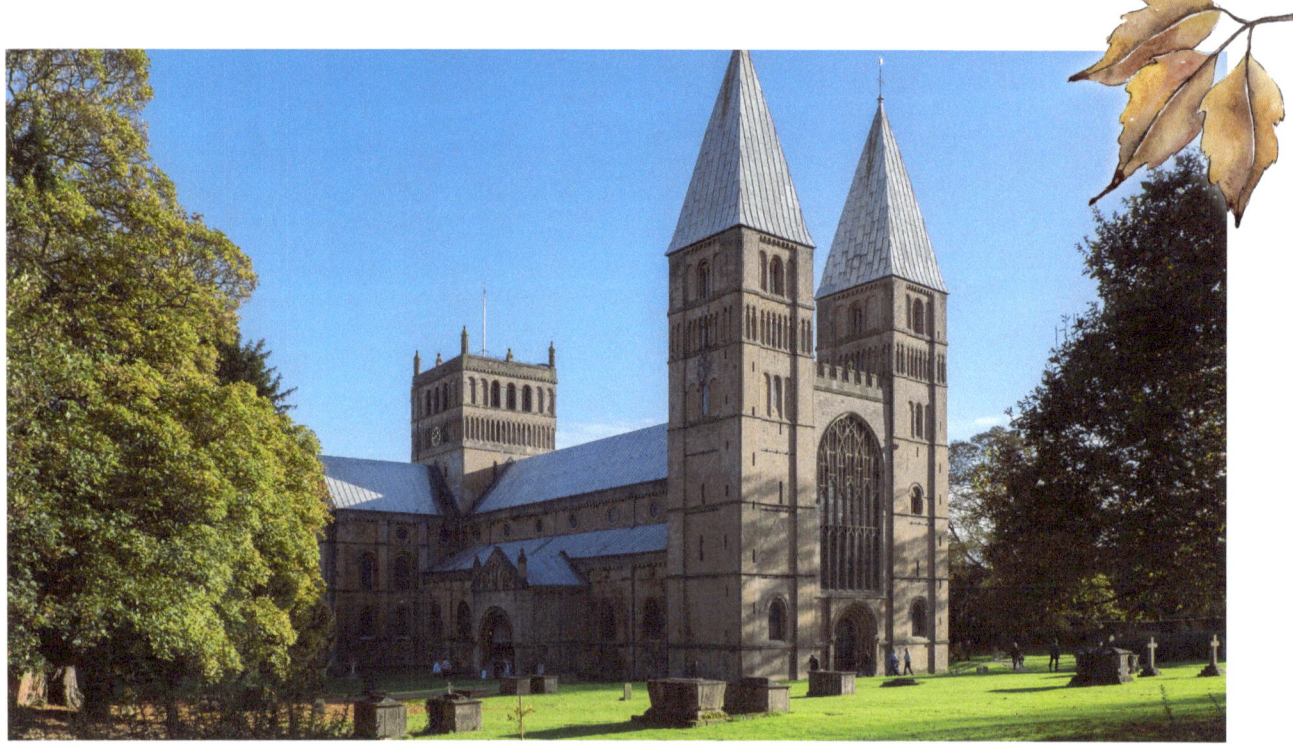

Construction of the Minster began in 1108 and lasted seventy years. It was a sort of sub-cathedral in the jurisdiction of York and held church authority over nearby Nottinghamshire.

The Chapter House, where the canons of the minster met to rule over matters of church business, is one of the most impressive examples of Gothic stonework in the British Isles. Covered with delicate and lifelike leaves and branches, the walls are like a garden turned magically to stone. And there, amid the hawthorn and oak leaves, are eleven foliated faces.

Southwell Minster's Canon Nigel Coates explains the Green Man's symbolism thusly: "In medieval times meetings of the college of canons would include a chapter of scripture which would be read and meditated on. Like the psalmist they would delight in God's law. The Green Man becomes an image that illustrates what happens when someone meditates, chews over that word of God. It leads to a verdant and fruitful life producing leaves that do not wither."

Four of the eleven Green Men in the Southwell Minster Charter House.

What About the Green Women?

As I walked slowly past the stone leaves, examining the faces in turn, I stopped in my tracks and stared at one face. I looked closer, considered carefully. The features did indeed appear feminine....

I exclaimed, "At last, here is a Green Woman!"

A knowedgeable Minster guide was standing nearby—I'd spoken with him earlier—and I said to him, "Wow! It's a Green Woman isn't it? I haven't seen one before."

Is this a Green Man or a Green Woman? What do you think?

Did Donald Trump have a twelfth-century doppelganger?

He replied, "Well . . . erm . . . some people think so." He paused a moment and then said, "Wouldn't you like to see a carving that we all think looks like your president Trump?"

He led us to that, and we agreed it did look like the Mr. Trump.

Point taken: it's easy to see resemblances that were never intended by the images' carvers.

Later, I found out that Canon Coates says the image in the Chapter House could "possibly" be a woman. More reading on the Internet led to the fact that this carving has traditionally been known as "the Oak King." (Despite the fact that those are acanthus leaves, not oak leaves, framing the face.)

My sister (who gave me my own Green Woman plaque) looked at a close-up photo of the Southwell foliated face and said, "It's a gender nonbinary Green Person."

My sister may be onto something. Some folklorists surmise that the foliated head images in the Chapter House harken back to legends of the fairies who live hidden in the forests—and portrayals of these forest spirits tend to be androgynous, indicating both their youth and unearthly essence. Given its setting, this Green Person could well be Puck the Faerie (of Shakespeare fame).

At any rate, now that I am well into my midlife, I have realized that there may be good reason to listen when people disagree with me—so I acknowledge that my Green Woman might be a Green Man. Or maybe Green Gender-Nonbinary.

Male or female? It may be that in some ways, the Green Spirit transcends gender.

The original image, in St. Bavo's Cathedral in Ghent, Belgium, appears above the archway into the crypt, the burial chamber, linking the image with the verdant leafy life that springs from death. But is this face masculine gendered?

But all this brings us back to the original question: why the Green *Man*? There are thousands of medieval Green Man carvings, and almost all of them are clearly male. If we are to uncover the truth of the soul of the Green Man, we must realize that medieval artists *were portraying a story or an idea that required male gender.*

Before we get to that, though, we need to further consider the Green Man's habitat.

While it's true that most Green Men are clearly male, some appear more androgynous, as with this medieval misericord carving.

A happy little Green Man taken from the ceiling of the cloisters of Durham Cathedral, where he and his seven brothers (all with very jolly expressions) serve as bosses covering the joints in the wood. The cloisters were built at the beginning of the fifteenth century, when the building was a monastery for Benedictine monks. Other bosses in the ceiling portray an angel, a frog, coats of arms, and flowers and leaves, indicating a vision of the world where the angelic hosts, the natural world, the political world, and human beings are all joined and intertwined.

5
The Green Man's Magical Medieval World

In 2011 Marsha and I had only a short time in Dublin and wanted to hit at least one old church. We learned we could make it to a service at Christ Church Cathedral, which has been a site of worship for over a thousand years. We got in just before the service began; afterward, the wardens promptly ushered us out, wanting to prepare the space for a soon-happening event. It wasn't an ideal way to explore a church, and we didn't see a Green Man.

We did, however, get a quick view of two neat details. One was the effigy tomb of the infamous Norman king Strongbow. In 1169, Strongbow and a thousand of his knights crossed over from England to fight for one Irish king against another.

He then married the daughter of the king for whom he was fighting and took over a good part of Ireland, which led to more than seven hundred years of English rule over the Irish. It was a bit of an odd feeling seeing the fearsome warrior king lying in effigy next to the pews.

But the thing that sticks out for me from that brief time in Christ Church was the floor tiles depicting a procession of foxy friars. The tiles are replicas of originals that covered this floor in the Middle Ages, showing foxes, walking upright, wearing hats and backpacks, and carrying walking sticks, like medieval pilgrims. The story

The foxy friars of Dublin's Christ Church Cathedral.

is that Christ Church became wealthy from the pilgrim trade, earning its keepers the appellation "foxy friars" for their skills at finagling tourists, a nickname that led to the tiles. Can you imagine any church nowadays putting pictures on their floor with animals dressed like the church staff? Or anything lampooning themselves? My takeaway was this: people in the Middle Ages had a good sense of humor and lively imagination.

Which brings us back to the Green Man. The medieval Green Man did not live alone; he dwelt beside other fantastic beings in a wonderfully strange, even outlandish, world, sharing an imaginal realm with creatures we now lump together as "mythical," including dragons, griffins, unicorns, angels, demons, pixies, ogres, and many more. Artists in the Middle Ages delighted in portraying these fantastic creatures in paintings, illuminated manuscripts, tapestries, carvings on church walls, and on wooden furniture. They populated residences, pubs, and churches.

One such being was the Woodwose, the Wild Man of the Woods. Like the Green Man, he is an archetypal figure, having lived for thousands of years

From left to right: The Church of St. Mary in Newbourne, Suffolk, has several carved Wodewoses; a medieval drawing depicts a Wodewose attacking a maiden; and this medieval woodcut hints at a closer relationship between the Green Man and the Wodewose, since it shows the Wodewose's connection to both the plant and animal worlds.

already in the folklore of the world before medieval masons thought to carve him. He harkens back to the hairy wild man Enkidu in the Gilgamesh Epic written in the Middle East before 600 BCE, and he lives on today in the popular image of Bigfoot. As the Green Man is the union of plant and human realms, the Wodewose is the union of animal and human realms.

Unlike the Green Man, the Wodewose is always full bodied (possessing a torso and all four limbs) and can be either male or female. Male Wodewoses are often portrayed grabbing maidens, an expression of their animalistic, unrestrained virility. The male Wodewose is frequently portrayed in combat with dragons and wild

64   *The Soul of the Green Man*

beasts, though he is shy and avoids humans. Unlike the Green Man, we know the Wodewose's name and we understand more about his identity because people in the Middle Ages wrote down his stories, giving us a clear and simple match-up between legends and images.

But other medieval beings lack good explanation. One such figure is the Sheela Na Gig. The meaning of her name is disputed; Sheela Na Gig may mean "hag on her haunches." She is a female exhibitionist, spreading herself for all to see. Sheela appears in some of the same churches as the Green Man. The Church of St. Mary and St. David in Kilpeck, Herefordshire, England, for example, is famous both for its Green Men and its Sheela. Like the Green Man, Sheela first appears after the Norman Invasion, and like the Green Man, she is a distinct and easily identified artistic image; the medieval masons had a clear idea what Sheela symbolized.

A Sheela from Rahara Church in Galway, Ireland.

The Green Man's Magical Medieval World

And yet, like the Green Man, Sheela is a mystery. Anyone in twelfth-century England would see her image and know who she was and what she meant, but no one (that we know of) wrote that down. There's been plenty of conjecture. Is she a continuing memory of the Great Mother Goddess, an archetype dating back to the Stone Age? Is she an assurance that God will be with women when they go through childbirth? Is she Eve, who gave birth to original sin? Is she a symbol of the "new birth" found in church, the visual, symbolic portrayal of Jesus' statement that we must "be born again"? Or is she a warning that wanton women will entice men into lust? Historians and folklorists have suggested all these sometimes-opposing theories as to Sheela's identity.

Sheela's presence on more than sixty churches in the British Isles reminds us that medieval people easily juxtaposed things we would call "bawdy" with things we would term "holy." The ease with which medieval people mixed sacred and profane (or, rather, what we nowadays divide into "sacred" or "profane") can be seen especially in medieval choir stall carvings. Sharing the same space as tonsured monks singing the Lord's praises were depictions of domestic brawls, nubile mermaids, biblical stories, pigs playing bagpipes, people drinking, knights fighting dragons, and even a man with his pants pulled down mooning the viewer.

The Middle Ages can serve as a mirror to understand our own times, and they tell us that we "permissive" moderns may be more uncomfortable with earthy realities than our ancestors a thousand years ago. People in the Middle Ages held an affirming view of ordinary life and the physical world—including *everything* in the phys-

Misericords in Wells Cathedral show a squatting man, a man with donkey ears, and a cat playing a fiddle.

ical world. The great Oxford scholar, theologian, and novelist C.S. Lewis, in his book *On English Literature in the Sixteenth Century*, describes the medieval mind in this way:

> *High abstractions and rarified artifices jostled the earthiest particulars. . . . They talked more readily than we about large universals such as death, change, fortune, friendship, or salvation; but also about pigs, loaves, boots, and boats. The mind darted more easily to and fro between that mental heaven and earth: the cloud of middle generalizations, hanging between the two, was then much smaller. Hence, as it seems to us, both the naivety and the energy of their writing. . . . They talk something like angels and something like sailors and stable-boys.*

One clue as to how people in the Middle Ages observed reality comes from bestiaries—books that included both real and allegorical creatures. These were medieval bestsellers. Between 200 CE and the thirteenth-century, writers and artists created more than a hundred different bestiaries. These included the African animals that were illustrated in the earliest Greek bestiary, as well as Northern fauna. From the perspective of folks living in the British Isles during the Middle Ages, the crocodile and the elephant were no less mysterious and amazing than the unicorn and the dragon. If readers had never seen an actual unicorn . . . well, most of them had never seen a lion or an ape, either. And each creature, whether familiar or otherworldly, had something important to say to the human heart and mind. The same creature often represented both Jesus and the devil, a paradoxical dichotomy that blurred dualistic black-and-white notions of good and evil. Each and every creature had some edifying symbolic meaning. The phoenix who rose from its ashes represented the resurrection of Christ. Bats navigate the dark because they have a God-given inner light that guides them through darkness.

And did you know rabbits ride on snails and have jousting events? There was a method to this madness; rabbits reminded medieval people that creatures that appear powerless can triumph over dominant forces in a society.

And then there's the bonnacon, which expels its dung in a noxious gas that can travel over two acres and burns anything it touches. (Wouldn't you like that card for a fantasy role-playing game?) In the medieval mind, even this has its illustrative purpose, a reminder that God protects creatures that humans regard as useless or unlikable.

The bonnacon is a beast with a head like a bull, but with horns that curl in toward each other. Because these horns are useless for defense, the bonnacon has another weapon: when pursued, the beast expels its dung in a noxious gas that travels a great distance (as far as two acres), and burns anything it touches. In this way God provides for the bonnacon, for God despises not that which humans regard as useless or unworthy.

Bestiaries give us an important clue to the "why" of the bizarre medieval portrayals of the world. *Every aspect of the physical world taught a lesson.* Nature was "God's first book." In the psalmist's words, "The heavens are telling the glory of God; and the firmament proclaims his handiwork. Day to day pours forth speech, and night to night declares knowledge" (Psalm 19:1 NRSV). Since natural objects could proclaim God's truths, things like stars, trees, and even stones were imbued with sentience. This perspective, a legacy of older beliefs, was supported by Scripture like this one: "For you shall go out in joy

The Green Man's Magical Medieval World

Rabbits and snails are the most harmless of animals, but we can imagine a topsy-turvy world where rabbits become warriors (and snails are their steeds). At first glance, this seems like a joke, but the reality is what Jesus shows us with his life: the victory of the less powerful over the dominant members of society, as well as the sheer joy and laughter of turning the world upside down. Warrior rabbits are a subversive symbol for all those who are downtrodden and weak in the eyes of the world.

A depiction of a monstrosity from an illuminated Bible. According to the medieval worldview, monstrosities live at the Earth's edges, where they come in many shapes and forms. They defy human-made boundaries and encourage us to regard them with fear but also with wonder and curiosity, daring us to see in them the parts of our own selves that lie outside the norm, parts we may keep concealed, even from ourselves.

and be led back in peace; the mountains and the hills before you shall burst into song, and all the trees of the field shall clap their hands" (Isaiah 55:12 NRSV).

The medieval world was therefore a magical and God-saturated place. Pigs and scullery maids, angels and demons, clouds, dragons, mice, and the service of Mass—all these things that seem oddly combined to our mind were unified in medieval thinking because they were all agents of God's self-revelation. In the Middle Ages, people refused to confine the Divine.

We may not be prone to decorating places of worship with such commonplace objects as people did eight hundred years ago, but we still see the sacred in Nature. The legendary Scottish-born naturalist John Muir said he'd rather be in the mountains thinking about God than in church wishing

The Green Man's Magical Medieval World   **71**

he were in the mountains—and that is also why I'm one of the facilitators for a local Forest Church gathering. Monthly, on a Saturday morning, a group meets at a trailhead or park and ventures into the wilds together to experience Spirit in the landscape, the trees, or the birds. We've gathered makings for wild teas, birdwatched with binoculars, trudged through snow, gathered fall leaves into patterns, and improvised chants around a blazing bonfire at night. In all these ways we still experience that sense of the Holy that people long ago perceived in Nature.

And what about our animal friends? Are they not agents of God's grace? I've learned as much about God's kindness from our dogs and cats as I have from humans. I know a woman whose life was saved by her cat, which persistently ran back and forth yowling to summon help when the cat's owner was fallen and unconscious. This woman said her cat was in fact an angel, and who am I to argue? The folks who carved the Green Man in

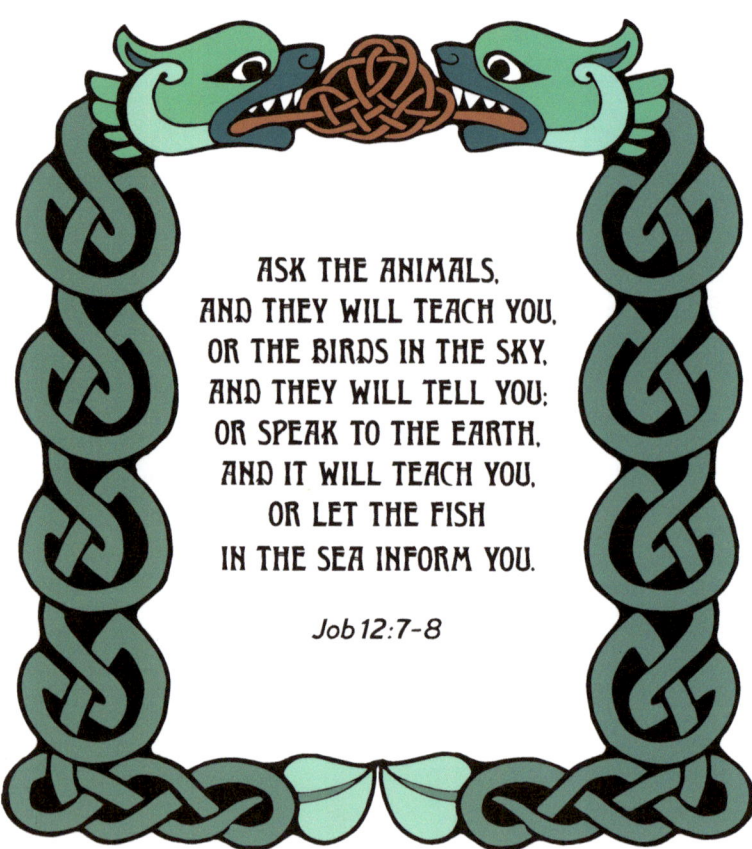

ASK THE ANIMALS,
AND THEY WILL TEACH YOU,
OR THE BIRDS IN THE SKY,
AND THEY WILL TELL YOU;
OR SPEAK TO THE EARTH,
AND IT WILL TEACH YOU,
OR LET THE FISH
IN THE SEA INFORM YOU.

Job 12:7-8

their churches and painted foxes on their floors shared this same sense of Divine presence in creatures.

And there are still places where holiness refuses to be pigeonholed. The Dalai Lama, regarded by millions of people as a model of enlightenment, can be seen on several YouTube videos laughing about inconvenient times to fart (that is, on airplanes, and while meditating with a group in silence). He even shifts his weight to share a bit of cheeky humor. As evidenced by their art, Europeans in the twelfth century would have appreciated his Holiness the Dalai Lama's earthy authenticity.

A bit later, in the fourteenth century, the famous mystic Julian of Norwich even saw Divine love and delight in the workings of our digestive system, including the rectum and anus. She wrote:

For God does not hold back from a single aspect of Creation, nor does the Divine One disdain to serve us in the simplest and most ordinary ways. Think how neatly our food is contained within our bodies, digested, and then is emptied out as needed, like a lovely drawstring purse that opens and closes. God is completely comfortable with all our bodies' activities; none of them offend the Divine Presence, for all our bodies' natural functions are Divine vehicles, filled with the love God bears us whose souls are made in the Divine likeness. (All Shall Be Well: A Modern-Language Version of the Revelation of Julian of Norwich, Anamchara Books)

The idea that the whole of reality is imbued with spiritual meaning can be termed sacramental. A sacrament, according to the website of U.S. Catholic bishops, has "a visible and invisible reality, a reality open to all the human senses but grasped in its God-given depths with the eyes of faith," and the specific sacraments defined by the Church include the Eucharist. The appearance of the Green Man in churches coincides with the timing of a new theological emphasis in the Western Christian tradition regarding the Eucharist: the real presence of Christ in the bread and wine.

Pope Gregory VII (who was Supreme Pontiff from 1073 to 1085) decreed "the bread and wine placed upon the altar are, by the mystery of the sacred prayer and the words of the Redeemer, substantially changed into the true and life-giving flesh and blood of Jesus Christ our Lord." At the same time, tales of the Holy Grail captured the Western imagination, fueling the sense of Divine magic filling the world.

In medieval times, religion soaked into every nook and cranny of daily existence. Believing that bread and wine were the actual salvation-giving body and blood of Christ, it wasn't hard to imagine that cows, clouds, and troubadours were also imbued with holy nature.

The Soul of the Green Man

Hildegard of Bingen (1098–1179) added to this perception of the God-infused physical realm. Hildegard was a German abbess, writer, musical and theatric composer, philosopher, mystic, and polymath. A dominant theme in her writings is *veriditas*, which translates to "greenness." Hildegard did not invent the term—it had been used by other theologians since the fourth century—but she was part of its growing popularity in the twelfth century. Theologically, the term indicated the understanding that as God creates and sustains the Earth, so God creates "new life" through Christ in human hearts and then causes this life to flourish.

A fifteenth-century portrayal of the Holy Grail at the center of King Arthur's Round Table.

The Green Man's Magical Medieval World

Veriditas—the greenness of Creation—points to God's presence in all things. This Divine inner essence allows both human and vegetative life to reproduce, grow, bring joy, and heal. One expression of Divine indwelling is the healing power of plants. Hildegard wrote, "O most honored Greening Force, You who roots in the Sun; You who lights up, in shining serenity, within a wheel that earthly excellence fails to comprehend. You are enfolded in the weaving of divine mysteries."

When I gaze into the Green Man's eyes, is the greening soul of Nature looking back at me?

Veriditas and the sacramental worldview of the twelfth century help us understand the larger world of the medieval imagination where salvation and pigs and Green Men mingle.

And while Hildegard helps us understand the Green Man's appeal in the twelfth century, a more recent scholar revolutionized our modern understanding of the Green Man. Let's journey on now for a meeting with Julia, Lady Raglan, in the first half of the twentieth century. It's like *Downton Abbey* meets the Green Man.

A rather dapper Green Man, sporting acanthus leaves, based on a twelfth-century image found in St. Mary de Crypt Church in Gloucester, England.

Lady Julia Introduces the Green Man to Society

Sometimes when I'm staring at a Green Man in an old church, I wonder, *What sorts of people have stood here in the centuries past and looked at this same fellow? What were their impressions?* Oh, to have a time machine!

I like to imagine an especially important encounter between a Green Man and Lady Julia Somerset, Duchess of Raglan, that occurred somewhere around 1931. The particular Green Man in question lives in the Church of St. Jerome Llangwm, a Norman era church in Pembrokeshire, Wales. He resides on an arch in the chancel (the part of a church where the priest serves communion). His meeting with a young folklorist changed Green Man history.

The parish church in Llangwm was mentioned for the first time in historical documents in 1128. It was renovated in the nineteenth-century, but much of the original ancient ornamentation remains.

I only know Lady Julia from a couple of portrait photos at the National Portrait Gallery and a few brief descriptions. I imagine her as someone like Lady Mary Crawley, the eldest daughter of an aristocratic (and fictional) family on the Masterpiece Theater television series *Downton Abbey*. Both Lady Julia and Lady Mary are fashionable, elegant, and self-assured; they take advantage of the greater opportunities afforded to their gender following the end of the first world war.

When she meets the Green Man, Lady Somerset is in her thirties and is married to Fitzroy Somerset Fourth Baron of Raglan. Both Raglans are members of the Folklore Society. Their ideas are influenced by other folklorists, including

This Green Man may be the one who impressed Lady Julia in the early twentieth century. He also has two brothers in the same church.

James Frazier and Jessie Weston. Frazier's *The Golden Bough: A Study in Comparative Religion* suggests that today's Western religions stem from ancient belief in a harvest god who marries the Goddess, and who dies and rises again, representing the seasonal cycles. Weston's *From Ritual to Romance: An Account of the Holy Grail from Ancient Ritual to Christian Symbol* extends Frazer's thinking to the Arthurian Grail legends. Both books continue to hold enormous influence in popular thinking about mythology and religion today, especially in the burgeoning revival of

This Green Man, based on a modern-day wall plaque, is immediately recognizable to us as a "Green Man"—but without Lady Julia's article, we would likely be giving him a different name. In fact, the Green Man might never have gained his place in our imagination without Lady Julia.

ancient Earth-based religions. Books on the Grail, from *The Mists of Avalon* to *The Da Vinci Code*, follow ideas in Weston's book.

All of this shapes the fertile ground in Lady Julia's imagination when the vicar of Llangwm church directs her attention to the Green Man. She is fascinated! She writes later, "It seemed to me certain that it was a man and not a spirit, and moreover that *it was a "Green Man." So I named it*" (italics mine). If she hadn't done this, today we probably wouldn't think of all these foliated heads as Green Men.

For the next eight years or so, Lady Julia went searching for the Green Man in Welsh and English churches, and then she published an article titled "The Green Man in Church Architecture." This article defined our modern-day ideas about the Green

Man in three important ways. Perhaps most important, before Lady Julia, writers just called our leafy friends "foliated heads."

Her second major impact was the assumption—based on intuition—that the foliated heads in medieval churches and the Jack in the Green who appears in folk dances were one and the same. She wrote, "I do not think that anyone who has seen these carvings can doubt that they are portraits." The sculptor, she believed, "copied what he saw" in the May Day rites of his time.

Finally, Lady Julia claimed to know the meaning of the Green Man. Riffing off the ideas of Frazer and Weston, she made a statement that has been echoed and expanded on ever since: "The fact is that unofficial paganism subsisted side by side with the official religion, and this explains the presence of the Green Man." According to this theory, our friend is the fertility god of ancient times, "the figure variously known as the Green

A modern-day Jack in the Green from a May Day celebration in Hastings in East Sussex.

Lady Julia Introduces the Green Man to Society **83**

Man, Jack-in-the-Green, Robin Hood, the King of May, and the Garland" and "Attis and Odin."

The Duchess of Raglan was an outstanding scholar of her time, but theories about history are constantly challenged, and her belief that the Green Man portrays officially forbidden Pagan deities is now out of favor among historians. Alex Woodcock, an archaeologist with a PhD, an authority on Romanesque architecture, and a stonemason, writes in his *Beakheads* blog that Lady Raglan's identification of the Green Man as an undercover Pagan deity succeeded:

What is the soul of the Green Man? If you ask Lady Julia, he is a pre-Christian fertility god, who has gone undercover to infiltrate Christian churches in the Middle Ages.

> *due in part to the prevailing opinion, during the middle decades of the twentieth century, of the medieval period as largely pagan. Accord-*

ing to this understanding the bulk of the people had remained true to their pagan roots, despite centuries of Christianity, the church allowing their imagery into its buildings as a means to pacify and ultimately convert them. Such an understanding was dismantled in the 1970s and '80s as detailed historical surveys were undertaken and published, which revealed medieval Christianity to be far more complex and nuanced than had previously been understood. But nonetheless, the idea of the Green Man as a pagan totem persisted and is by far the most popular interpretation today.

This Green Man is inspired by a doorknocker in Derbyshire, England.

Still, we owe a huge debt to Lady Julia—and her ideas make me wonder: What *were* the Green Man's roots? It's time to take a look at the Green Man's family tree.

Lady Julia Introduces the Green Man to Society

This Green Man was originally drawn by Hans Sebald Beham, a German printmaker who lived from 1500 to 1550.

The Family Tree

Since Lady Raglan, there's been much written about the ancient roots of the Green Man's family tree, tracing his descent from ancient Nature deities and images from the Classical world. I look at pictures of these pre-medieval "Green Men," and I look at the faces in Gothic sanctuaries and wonder, "Was that really your great-great-great grandfather?"

When researching roots and relations, one must be cautious. Just because people look like they're related, doesn't make it so. In the town where I used to live there was a man who looked just like me, and we shared a friendship and common social circles. He was a teacher at a local school, and I worked for a time with the students in that school's creative writing course. One day I stepped into his classroom as he was about to step out and I agreed to watch the class for a few minutes; students were busy and didn't notice the exchange. A minute later one of his students walked up to the desk and started talking—he was looking right into my face, just a few feet away—going on and assuming I was his regular teacher. That's how close the resemblance was. People referred to us as "twins," though there was no blood relation between us, a reminder that resemblance doesn't prove family identity.

And if you've done much genealogy work you know how easily you can get off on the wrong branch researching the family tree. Let's say you are a Jones from Wales. You come upon a record of Ann and John Jones who had a daughter, Emily, in 1902. And you know that your great-grandmother was Emily Jones, born in Wales, in 1902. It's tempting to mark down another generation on the family tree, assuming Ann and John are the next generation going back in time. But, wait! Although this seems like an obvious connection, there were a surprising number of Jones from Wales, and there can be several Emilys born the same year. After more research, you discover a photocopy of your Emily Jones's baptismal record and you see that her parents were Richard and Evi—not Anne and John. Oops! This sort of mistake is common when people try to trace their family tree.

Likewise, we must be careful connecting dots in the Green Man's lineage. There are two easily made mistakes. First is the assumption that one artistic creation must be the inspiration for another. It's possible for artists to create similar motifs with-

This carving from Hatra, Iraq, may depict the ancient Mesopotamian folk figure Humbaba, Lord of the Cedar Woods. It does resemble the foliated heads that Norman stonemasons carved on medieval churches, but there may be no direct historical link between them.

out any influence or knowledge of a previous artist's work; this has happened repeatedly throughout history.

Even if one image influences the artistic form of another, it's possible that the meaning of images has changed over time. A craftsman in the Romanesque era of the Middle Ages may copy the shape of a foliated head from ancient Roman times but have no idea what that image meant to a craftsman a thousand years earlier. The medieval artist would ascribe an entirely different name and symbolic meaning to that image, having no knowledge of the name and symbolism ascribed by the Roman era artist.

With that in mind, let's look at images that are similar to the later Green Man. As well as the ancient Middle Eastern figure Humbaba, there are also later Middle Eastern Green Men that have a strong visual resemblance to the medieval foliated heads.

The Family Tree

This floor mosaic (on display in the Istanbul Museum) from the late Roman era shows a foliated head that looks suspiciously like a Green Man—and yet its symbolism was likely quite different from that intended by Western Europeans several centuries later.

We can also find family resemblance to the Green Man in sources geographically closer to his later medieval home, in the ancient art of the Celtic people. The Pfalzfeld pillar, from the fifth century BCE, for example, shows a head with shapes emerging from it that may be leaves. Whatever the exact meaning may have been, it's likely that the carving indicates the veneration of ancient Celtic peoples for disembodied heads.

Disembodied heads held great power within ancient Celtic thought. According to the Welsh myth cycle *The Mabinogion*, when the warrior-hero Bran was mortally

After more than two thousand years, the exact meaning of this leafy head carved on the Pfalzfeld pillar has been lost. It is likely that it portrayed some form of superhuman or divine being. The Celts believed that the head was the seat of the human soul and therefore a source of magical power. Ancient Celtic legends relate the importance of taking enemies' heads in battle and displaying them as trophies. The Celtic practice of head-taking was practiced into the onset of the Christian era.

wounded, he asked his fellows to cut his head off, telling them to take the head with them and it would continue to dispense wisdom. They did so, and the head fulfilled its promise. Eventually, the head was buried in London, where it protected Britain from invaders. The tradition of Bran's head continues to today, as ravens are kept at the tower of London and many tourists hear the story that if the Tower of London ravens are lost or fly away, the Crown will fall and Britain with it. Bran in the old Celtic tongues means "raven," and the ravens are a remembrance of Bran's head protecting the Isle.

The Grail myth also holds resonances of the Celtic cult of the severed head. Originally, the Grail was not a chalice but a platter, and in one Welsh version of the story, the Grail holds a severed head, reminiscent of

The Family Tree

Bran's head. It is tempting to see echoes of the Celtic head cult in the Green Man's appeal through medieval times, though such a connection is merely speculative.

In the centuries before and after Christ "all roads lead to Rome." From the time of Julius Caesar up until the collapse of the Roman empire, Latin governance, customs, and art dominated the Western world, and for a thousand years after the fall of Rome, European culture attempted to re-create Roman standards. So, when looking at any icon of the Middle Ages—such as the Green Man—it would make sense to look for Roman roots in the family tree. And there are in fact Roman images that bear a strong resemblance to the Green Man.

This image of the River God Achelous, based on a Roman floor mosaic in Turkey, looks very much like the Green Men found in Gothic churches a millennium later.

This second-century Roman mosaic also looks very much like a foliated head. It portrays, however, the sea god Neptune. (Those are crab claws emerging from his head.)

This image, based on a carving from the ancient hot baths in Bath, England, is often cited as a Roman-era Green Man. It's also a good example of how ambiguous the meaning of art can be, since the figure's beard and hair have been explained variously as serpents, sunbeams, seaweed, or foliage.

This acanthus-sprouting head is based on a carving that dates back to the first century. It was originally found in Rome and is now in the Musée de Vésone, Périgueux, Dordogne, France. The image has been identified as Pan, the god of Nature who connects the Divine with the natural world. There are numerous examples of these "leaf faces" from the Classical World. They appear to be leaves pressed into the contours of human visage—not so much vegetable-human hybrids, as vegetation mimicking human form.

The tendrils of the Green Man's family tree extend from the ancient Hellenistic world through the Byzantine era. The Byzantine era links the time between ancient Rome and the Middle Ages; this was when the Roman Empire had moved from the banks of the Tiber to the city of Constantinople (named after the Roman Emperor Constantine, responsible for the conversion of the Roman Empire to Christianity). Constantinople was also known as Byzantium, and today is Istanbul, Turkey. Could the foliated heads found from this era have helped to shape the Green Man we know and love?

As we continue to climb up the Green Man's (speculative) family tree, we find ourselves in the Early Middle Ages. The greatest art form of this period was illuminated sacred texts. As the Latin alphabet and reverence for the Bible spread into newly Christianized lands, ancient Celtic and Gemanic designs com-

A Green Man from the Byzantine era can be found on the Tomb of St. Abre (4th–5th century CE) now in the Church of St. Hilaire-le-Grand at Poitiers, France. If this Green Man was secretly inserted into the interior of a Norman church, no one would think it out of place; it's a perfect example of a foliated face. It's also very unusual during this time frame—only a few examples of Green Men from this historical period have been identified.

bined with the artistic heritage of Greece and Rome, flowering in extraordinary works of paint, gilding, and ink on velum (parchments made from animal skins).

Today, tourists wait in line to see the Book of Kells in Trinity Library and reproductions of the artwork abound. I love to get lost in a book with full-size glossy pages reproduced from the Book of Kells or the equally amazing Lindisfarne Gospels. The designs seem almost infinitely complex and interwoven: motifs from Middle Eastern carpets, Roman mosaics, Neolithic temples, and Byzantine churches join in a wildly flowing and brightly colored dance. And the Green Man—or his cousins—does emerge from some of the pages of these Early Middle Ages tomes.

Here, I feel confident that we have a link in the Green Man's family tree. These Green Men that appear in the Book of Cerne and Codex Egberti are similar to the

The Family Tree

These two Green Men flank the eagle, the symbol of John's Gospel, in the Book of Cerne, a ninth-century Anglo-Saxon prayer book, whose pages include Celtic, Anglo-Saxon, and Mediterranean influences.

In the later medieval period, illuminated manuscripts continued to offer a medium for scribes' fertile imagination, a playground where fancy and spiritual insight could mingle and dance. Here (from left to right) we see a Green Man with a dragon or gryphon's body, a full-bodied Green Man who's perhaps intended to be a version of Wodewose, and a Green Man riding a Green Horse. All three images give us a sense of a world where the human spirit and the spirits of plants and animals merge, all within a scriptural setting.

Green Men on the baptismal font in Brecon Cathedral—perhaps carved at the same time as the Codex Egberti was manufactured—and they also bear a resemblance to the Green Men at Kilpeck (which we'll visit in the next chapter). These Green Men appear in the context of Christian faith, and there is artistic continuity from the Byzantine period into the later Middle Ages.

It's likely that some of the Green Men who appear so commonly in Norman churches during the Middle Ages are in fact artistic reproductions of images pro-

If you look at the very bottom center of this image, you'll see a small version of our friend the Green Man. This is a page from the Codex Egberti, which was produced in the tenth century at Reichenau Monastery and is now housed at the city library of Trier, Germany.

The Soul of the Green Man

duced in the ancient Roman world. But remember a point made in the beginning of this chapter: *Even if one image influences the artistic form of another, it's possible that the meaning of images has changed over time.* I very much doubt that a stone mason in the eleventh-century, seeing a Roman mosaic with a foliated head, would think, "I'll just carve a Roman river god into the chancel of this church." He may have been inspired by the art and moved to create his interpretation of that leafy visage, but he wouldn't necessarily know the words and stories that went with that artistic inspiration. He'd more likely think about the foliated face in terms of stories and symbols prevalent in his own time.

So we may have found the inspiration for the *artistic form* of the Green Man, but we haven't yet gotten to the root of *meaning* in the medieval Green Man. For this, we will have to investigate further.

The Green Man's story has on occasion merged with the legend of the Green Knight.

The Green Man in King Arthur's Court

Do you have any odd relatives in your family? You know, the ones who make gatherings so much more interesting, and then provide occasion for more talk after they are gone? The Green Knight, a character from Arthurian legend, may be the Green Man's crazy relative—at least some medievalists think so. But he's as fearsome as he is amusing.

Speaking of weird relatives, some family members might think that's—*ahem*—me. If so, I blame my parents for encouraging me to read and letting me follow my own interests. In elementary school, I got into Arthurian mythology and it hooked me. It also played no small role in the strange interests I still pursue in adulthood.

Have you ever seen something that seemed both strange *and* familiar? That would be the definition of an oxymoron, but that's what I found as a boy reading the legends of the Round Table. Characters had such outlandish ideas, the names were unfamiliar, and events happened randomly. Knights ride into dark tangled forests just on a whim, where they meet hermits and strange women and shape-shifting beings. They are given riddles or dares. Sometimes the stories end but give no explanation for events, either for the reader or for the characters in the stories. Although these tales were odd, reading them as a child, I felt like I belonged in these stories. They were easy to imagine and, having glimpsed the imaginary realms of Camelot and Albion, I wanted to enter in and stay.

I asked my father why I felt both captivated and mystified by Arthurian legends and he said to me, "Kenneth, these are the stories of our people from long ago. *They tell us who we are.*" In the years since then I've earned a degree in English, then an advanced degree in religion and have taught in college about ideas like "archetypes" and "the hero's journey." And in all that time, the best definition of *myth* is the explanation my father gave me so long ago. Myths are the stories "that tell us who we are."

That explains how a story can be both strange and familiar. Celtic and medieval legends seem strange because they occur in a world so distant from our own, in time, culture, and language; yet they speak to us in our soul (*psyche* is the Greek word for soul). They communicate to our subconscious and ancestral memories, and hence wield great power.

One such tale is that of the Green Man's purported family member, the Green Knight. He is as bizarre as any character in the strange Arthurian realm, literally

This N. C. Wyeth 1922 illustration from The Boy's King Arthur: Sir Thomas Malory's History of King Arthur and His Knights of the Round Table *shows the Green Knight as merely a knight dressed in green. Note, however, that his horn is chained to a tree, indicating a connection to the growing green world.*

bigger than life, an enigma even to the other characters in the medieval tale.

He is already old before he appears in the tale of *Sir Gawain and the Green Knight,* written in the late Middle Ages. A pre-Christian Irish tale of the hero Cuchullain tells of a shape-shifting mage named Cu Roi, which follows a similar plot as the later medieval tale. Although the collections of tales about Arthur and his companions were written during the Norman era and afterward, the characters, plots, and devices in these tales often harken from the mists of the deep Celtic past.

The tale of the Green Knight proceeds thusly: A strange and terrible being rides into Arthur's court amid the Round Table Yuletide feast; he is a giant. "And all garbed in green this giant and his gear. In his one hand he held a holly branch, that is greatest in green when groves are bare, and an axe in his other, one huge, monstrous." He issues a challenge to exchange blows—which Sir Gawain accepts. When Gawain cuts off the Green Knight's head, the green giant picks up his severed head, puts it back in place, and tells Gawain to meet him in a year hence so that the Green Knight can deliver his blow to Gawain's neck.

Sean Connery played the Green Knight in the movie, Sword of the Valiant.

Spring and summer come and go; then, after All Hallows' Day, Gawain, "for good known, and, as purified gold, void of every villainy, with virtues adorned," embarks to meet the Green Knight and fulfill his half of the bargain. Gawain wanders through tangled woods, combats dragon, wolf, and Wodewose, sleeps in the rain and on the frosted ground, praying to Mary all along the way.

Eventually he arrives at a resplendent castle where the porter greets him with hospitality, and he feasts sumptuously in a rich hall. The lord of the castle is most gracious,

The original medieval manuscript that tells the story of Sir Gawain and the Green Knight.

and the lady of the castle is breathtakingly beautiful. There is also an old hag in the castle.

The lord tells Sir Gawain that the Green Knight's chapel is nearby. He invites Gawain to stay and rest before his encounter with the Green Knight, also inviting Gawain to a game: they will part during each day and at day's end they will exchange whatever they happen to obtain during the day. Gawain agrees to this.

Each day the lord of the castle goes hunting and harvests his prey, and each day the beautiful lady presses herself on Gawain. He is tempted to sin, but the Virgin Mary protects Gawain as reward for his prayers. On the first day, the lady of the castle kisses him, and Gawain passes that on to her husband in the evening. The second day, she gives him a brace of kisses, which he also passes on. Then on the third day, the lady gives him three kisses and a magical green woven belt, which she promises will protect him. Gawain in turn passes the three kisses to his host, but he does not mention the magical garland.

Lud's Chapel, a narrow, leafy ravine in England's Peak District, is, according to tradition, the site of Gawain's meeting with the Green Knight.

On New Year's morning Gawain and his hosts sadly part, and he makes his way to the Chapel of the Green Knight, which is overgrown with vegetation, dark and ill boding. The Green Knight greets Gawain and congratulates his integrity in keeping their appointment. Gawain prepares himself for the Green Knight's axe: "Strike but the one stroke, and I shall stand still and offer no hindrance, come work as you like, I swear."

The first two axe blows, the Green Knight pulls short of Gawain's neck, and on the third strike he only cuts Gawain slightly. Then, the Green Knight reveals that he is the lord of the Castle who has been Gawain's host. He withheld the first two blows because Gawain was completely honest on the first two days of their daily exchange, and the slight cut is because Gawain was honest about the kiss but not the green belt. The Green Knight embraces Gawain and invites him back to the castle for revels. Gawain presses for the knight's name, and he reveals himself as Sir Bertilak, along with the fact that the old hag in the castle is "the Goddess Morgan," who forced Bertilak and his lady to play their respective roles in the drama. Gawain returns to Arthur's court and tells his story; Arthur decrees that the Knights of the Round Table shall each wear a green sash as memento of this amazing adventure.

It's typical of Arthurian myth, both strange and compelling. There's obviously a lot going on beneath the surface of this tale. John Matthews, the master of Arthurian and Celtic lore, says in his book *The Arthurian Tradition*, "In the story of Gawain and the Green Knight the contest becomes a test of Gawain's purity and honor as well as a reflection of the Christian concept of redemption and renewal." He also notes the importance of Morgan the Goddess, noting, "Such figures are an essential part of the inner dimension of the tradition. They are the initiators who cause things to happen, leaving the neophyte changed forever after."

The tale of the Green Knight came to my mind when I was visiting the Parish Church of St. Mary and St. David in Kilpeck, Herefordshire, which shares that same strange and compelling, myth-infused character. The Welsh border region in its entirety is a liminal place—an in-between landscape where modernity and history, fact and legend, English and Celtic, hill and village all intersect. Since Roman times, differing cultures with their passions, hatreds, and tales, have mated and killed, merged and contested there.

It was a lovely spring day as Marsha and I drove up to the Kilpeck Church. I'd long wished to see this rural marvel of Romanesque art and was not disappointed. The church was built beside the local Norman castle, but now that keep is reduced to a picturesque ruin atop a grassy motte and bailey; when we were there, a flock of sheep grazed beneath the fallen ramparts. The land was already sacred before these buildings were erected: the castle and church were built near springs, ancient yews, and on a ley line.

The Kilpeck Church in Herefordshire.

The church is an artistic tour-de-force, with the doorway, arches, windows, and eaves ornately carved with intertwining and fantastical images. It is representative of the Hereford School of architecture, which incorporates Celtic, Saxon, Viking, and French motifs. The church is dedicated to the Virgin Mary and St. David of Wales, reflecting the Welsh-Norman character of the Marches. It's a wild menagerie and pastiche of early-medieval life, with magical

Some of the Kilpeck Church carvings: (from left to right), a birdman, a man playing a fiddle, and a Sheela Na Gig.

creatures like manticores and ouroboroses and a head disgorging serpents, along with people making music and dancing, a dog and a hare, and an iconic Sheela. It seems as if the lord of the adjacent castle wanted his chapel to contain as much embellishment as that contained in nearby Hereford Cathedral.

The prevalence of Nature motifs brings the outdoors into the church—or vice-versa, while the surreal style of the figures creates a "thin place" suspended between mundane reality and legend. The exterior of the church seems situated in the faerie realm, whereas the inside is a peaceful and enfolding Christian space, dominated by Christ's apostles. As I walked slowly around the church and then inside, I could easily imagine the Norman lords and ladies and knights of the castle, along with Welsh peasants of the land, who lived in a world of strange powers, of Nature and magic intermingled. Entering the church, they passed from the realm of powers, both military and supernatural, to observe the renewing power of the Eucharist.

And there are Green Men. The most notable is the "greeter" on the column to the right of the doorway. He's hardly a friendly, welcoming greeter, and I hesitate to say "Green *Man*" insofar as this figure is something more-than-human. He is more of a mask, or a spirit, a being from another realm radiating fearsome power.

Otherworldly and imposing, this Green Man shares the spirit of the Green Knight. And yet, I'm not sure they are the same. The Green Knight and this outlandish foliated head share connections with the natural and magical realms—but did the medieval storyteller intend a connection with the same Green Man we see in churches? It's hard to tell. In the

The foliage that erupts from the mouth of the Kilpeck Church's doorway Green Man appears to be rope or beadwork and extends into leaves and a cluster of grapes.

first written account, the Green Knight is described as:

> Well garbed was this giant geared in green, and the hair of his head like his horse's mane. Fair fanned-out flax enfolds his shoulders; a beard big as a bush over his breast hangs.

The references to "flax" and "bush" are vegetative, but there's no mention of leaves or tendrils from his mouth or nose or ears. So—is the Green Knight a Green Man? I leave the reader to decide. For now, let's turn our attention to another tradition that may bear some relation to our foliated friend.

This unusual full-bodied Green Man, based on a carving from a choir stall in Winchester Cathedral, bears a sword and a shield, indicating that his creator might have seen some connection between the Green Man and the Green Knight.

The Green Man in King Arthur's Court

The symbolism of the maypole has been continuously debated by folklorists for centuries, but no definitive answer has been found. Some scholars have suggested that maypoles are symbols of the sacred World Tree from Germanic Pagan beliefs, and other scholars have seen phallic symbolism in them. Most historians today, however, believe that maypoles originated during Christianity, in the fourteenth century. The anthropologist Mircea Eliade theorized that the maypoles were simply a part of the general rejoicing at the return of summer and the growth of new vegetation, with their shape allowing for garlands and greenery to be hung from them.

Jack and the Maypole

How many calendar dates in your life can you remember, years later? "On that day I was at such-and-such" or "I was with so-and-so." You doubtless recall dates like the birth of a child, a wedding, the funeral of a loved one, or perhaps significant birthdays. I'll always remember where I was on May 1, 2016.

My wife Marsha, our friend and editor Ellyn, and I were staying in a rambling medieval house in Devon, England, where we were vaca-working on writing business. I was excited to be in Southern England as Beltane approached. (May Day, formerly known by its Celtic name Beltane, was one of the Celts' chief festivals, marking the beginning of summer.) I had done my research, and there were two events I wanted to attend.

May Day morning, we started out at the magical hour of 3:30 and drove over an hour between hedge rows through unlit roads, arriving in the chilly pre-dawn at Haytoor Rocks in Dartmoor. Dartmoor is one of the strangest, most haunting environments in England, both barren and lovely. Its desolate moors and dramatic rock escarpments seem like a Mars-scape at times, and Wistman Wood with its moss-covered dwarf oaks is the perfect enchanted forest. No wonder Arthur Conan Doyle placed his story "The Hound of the Baskervilles" in Dartmoor.

Dartmoor at dawn is a magical and mysterious place.

Beneath the craggy granite outcropping at Haytoor Rocks we gathered with a small crowd of folks to celebrate the Beltane dawn with Morris dances. The place is so isolated that the dances were done right in the middle of the road—and not a car came by to interrupt. There were three dance troupes there, with their attendant musicians. Onlookers were friends or family of the dancers. Part of the excitement of being there was the sense that this was not a performance—at least not performance for a human audience. I experienced the dances as *ritual*, enacted for the land, the rising sun, the ancestors.

No one is certain where we get the expression "Morris dance." Some suggest the word derives from the medieval word "Moorish" (Muslim), but that is by no means certain. We know these dances are older than the Reformation, because Protestants protested them—but how far

These Morris dancers are referred to as "crows," recalling the ancient connection between corvids and the deities of the land: the Morrigan, who shape-shifted to crow; Bran the demigod, whose name means "raven"; and Wotan the one-eyed All-Father with his two ravens "memory" and "awareness."

Jack and the Maypole

back in history are their origins? Julia Somerset and other folklorists point to the Morris dance tradition as a survival of pre-Christian rites having to do with both fertility and the resurrection of new life out of death. Some Morris dancers hold up deer's antlers as they dance—why? No one remembers, but customs like that seem to give credence to an origin in the ancient Nature religion.

A modern-day Jack in the Green joins the revelry at a Morris dance.

One of the troupes on this May Day morning was the Beltane Border Morris group. They performed in blackface—recalling the prominence of chimney sweeps in May Day celebrations of the eighteenth and nineteenth centuries—and wore long shredded strips of black fabric. Their dance was combative; rows of dancers whirled and charged one another, screaming what can only be described as battle cries, and clashing hardwood sticks so roughly that chips flew. It was dance, sport, and melee in one. Those folklorists who are inclined to see ancient fertility rituals in the dance will point to this as ritual combat between the forces of winter and of summertime, performed on Beltane as summer engages in climactic and victorious battle against cruel and resistant winter.

May Day Green Men in all their leafy wonder.

And as another Morris troupe danced, a vegetative figure strode into their midst—our friend Jack in the Green! He was wearing a camouflage ghillie suit, designed for soldiers and hunters, and a leaf-face mask patterned after the classic foliated heads in churches, and he carried an unmistakably phallic staff. He served as a human maypole, standing amid the dancers whose movements swirled round about him. While his outfit was modernized, this Jack in the Green was rooted in countless leafy ancestors who have appeared on May Day mornings in centuries past, an icon of summer greenery once again filling the land.

After the dance troupes finished their choreographed rituals, the rest of us were invited to join the revelries. A dancer handed us hardwood sticks, and they showed us how to dance in opposing circles, whacking our sticks against one another. We entered into the dance, gingerly batting with the staffs, gleeful as we joined the ancient rite.

And then, when the dawn had driven darkness off the moors and crags, the crowd dispersed. The roadside that was filled with accordion music, the clash of sticks, and loud shouts, was lonely and silent again. Marsha, Ellyn, and I drove north to Glastonbury for our second Beltane celebration of the day.

We arrived before festivities began and relaxed in a warm coffee shop with papier-maché dragons in the window display. I ordered a coffee with whisky, just the thing to restore warmth internally. Then we explored the streets of this medieval town, with its crystal shops, bookshops, and a store called The Green Man and the Goddess.

Glastonbury Tor is an ancient site of myth and magic.

Glastonbury is a myth magnet—a town that has attracted the legends of the Goddess, Merlin, Saint Patrick, Saint Brigid, and King Arthur all into one place. To disparagers, it is woo-woo-ville, where competing reincarnations of King Arthur stand on crates while young people beat drums by the Market Cross. Yet it has always been a place of myth, both Pagan and Christian. The Chalice Well with its lovely grounds and ancient yews can claim continuity with the same springs venerated as holy before Rome's legions entered its environs. The Tor may be a pre-Christian ritual site, the navel of ancient Avalon, and the Abbey—while perhaps not actually founded by Joseph of Arimathea, as was claimed by its medieval bishops—was built atop one of Britain's most

The ancient past lies dreaming amid the ruins of Glastonbury Abbey.

ancient churches. A sign on the Abbey Grounds marks the spot where the graves of Arthur and Guinevere were allegedly unearthed in the Middle Ages, an attempt to put to death rumors that the once-and-future-king would rise to lead a Welsh rebellion against Norman overlords. The George and Pilgrims Inn, still serving travelers in the midst of the town, has done so since the time when Chaucer wrote Canterbury Tales.

Crowds began to gather . . . and gather and gather. Soon the quaint medieval streets were crammed full of modern celebrants, shoulder-to-shoulder. Glastonbury's Beltane festival is not a reenactment of May Days past but a contemporary celebration of annual renewal. Two human-filled life-sized dragons (if "life-sized" can rightly apply to fantasy beasts), like the dragons in Chinese New Year's, danced through the streets. There were dramas (though I could not fight through the crowds to get the gist of them). And there were Green Men. Lots of Green Men.

The Green Men carried the maypole—a sizable trunk—into the town square, then up a long hill to the field where it was erected and festooned. A May Queen and May King were "married." The May King was costumed as the Green Man.

Marsha, Ellyn, and I were "green" versions of ourselves in honor of the May Day festivities in Glastonbury.

Clearly, the Green Man is a ubiquitous symbol of this modern continuation of the ancient Beltane rites. Renewal of the old Celtic Nature religions has emphasized the importance of the Green Man as a symbol of Beltane, and modern dancers dressed as Jack in the Green design their outfits to resemble the medieval foliated faces. This reinforces Lady Raglan's assumption that leaf-faces-in-churches and Jack-in-the-Green May-Day dancers are one and the same.

But . . . Jack in the Green in preceding centuries didn't look like these modern Green Men. When I see pictures of

The traditional Jack in the Green of yesteryear did not look much like a Green Man at all!

a traditional Jack in the Green, I'm reminded of Monty Python's *Holy Grail* and the knights who say "Neek," when they command King Arthur, "Bring us . . . a shrubbery!" A historical May Day Jack in the Green, enclosed in a series of hoops covered with leaves, looks like walking shrubbery—or a Christmas tree with a pair of feet and eyes poking through the green.

The earliest documentation of a May Day Jack in the Green is 1770, and throughout the past two and a half centuries, Jack in the Green has been linked with the guilds of chimney sweeps, appearing on May Day with a troupe of men and women sweeps, their faces blackened denoting their trade, engaging in bawdy song and gesture and asking for donations from passers-by.

Black-face Morris dancers have sparked controversy in recent years, since in today's world, black-face has been used as a racist statement against people of African descent. Morris dancers insist that the tradition predates racism against Africans and instead celebrates outlaws and chimney swifts, those who live outside society's normal boundaries. This man's combination of black and green face paint indicates a connection between societal rebellion and the world of the forest. (See chapter 10 on Robin Hood.)

With the more refined sensitivities of the Victorian and Edwardian ages, Jack in the Green began to disappear from May Day festivities, but the burgeoning growth of Nature religions in the twenty-first century has resulted in a multitude of Jacks in the Green dancing on May Day throughout England. (For those interested in a more thorough write-up of Jack in the Green and folklore traditions, I recommend *The Green Man in Britain* by Fran & Geoff Doel.)

When we try to understand his message, Jack in the Green presents the same difficulty that we encounter with the leaf faces in churches: a lack of explanation in historical texts. The revelries of the peasantry didn't receive a great deal of attention in the writings of the Middle Ages, and when folkloric rituals do appear in old texts, knowledge by the reader is assumed rather than explained. Adding to the difficulty in understanding, it is hard

This early seventeenth-century fellow looks more like the leafy faces in churches, as opposed to the walking Christmas-tree that is Jack in the Green. But does he have any connection with May Day? Or any connection with leaf faces in churches?

to discern which elements in Morris dances and May Day rituals are ancient customs that have been passed on mouth-to-mouth, and which are modern interpretations.

The appellation "Green Man" coupled with staged events predates the eighteenth-century documentation of Jack in the Green. The script for a play titled *Historie of Promos and Cassandra*, published in 1578, includes the entry of two men "appareled lyke greene men at the mayor's feast with clubs of fireworks." We can make the likely guess that these characters looked like the illustration of a Green Man with a firework club published five decades later (shown above).

As I stood in the cold dawn of that Beltane morning, watching the Morris dancers and their friend Jack in the Green, I felt a palpable sense of continuity with the ancient past. I realize that when I taught comparative religions in college—where all statements had to be made with the precision of academia—my intuitions about Jack would not

Jack and the Maypole

have flown far. And yet, while some folklorists today are inclined to reject the beliefs of Julia Somerset and her peers regarding the pre-Christian origins of Morris dances and Jack in the Green, I wonder.

Those dancers silhouetted before the rising of the sun on this chilly morning, liminal between winter and summer, seemed to echo a primordial heritage.

Unlike the carved foliated faces, Jack appears in festivities that were performed outside of churches, and were not connected with explicitly Christian rites. The dour Reformers of the sixteenth and seventeenth centuries apparently had no objection to the foliated visages in their places of worship—but they did rail heartily against May Day celebrations. And Jack in the Green, clad in deciduous leaves, appeared for centuries precisely on the first day of summer (according to the ancient Celtic seasonal reckoning). Can all that be coincidence?

Doesn't Jack, in all his leafiness, say to us, "No matter how bitter the winter, new life will come again"? Green will rise from the Earth, babies will be conceived and born, and Nature will repeat her endless cycle of renewal.

On Dartmoor at dawn, I looked into the eyes of the Jack in the Green, and he seemed to wink at me saying, "I am the symbol of your ancestors' faith in the summertime renewal of the land."

But is that message the Green Man's secret? I'm not so sure. Certainly, there's something of the rascal about him, which puts him akin not only to the modern-day Jacks in the Green but also that most beloved of all outlaws—Robin Hood.

Taken from a modern Green Man on display in Sherwood Forest.

The Green Man and His Merry Men

One afternoon in childhood, I was at my aunt's house watching a black-and-white television set with my cousins, when the 1938 Errol Flynn movie *The Adventures of Robin Hood* happened to be playing. I loved it! How he leapt and swung and tricked the sheriff's men, how he stood up for the little people, all with that look of absolute joy on his face. That night and the days following, I played Robin Hood with a hastily contrived wooden sword.

Soon after, my parents bought me the Golden Press edition of Howard Pyle's *The Merry Adventures of Robin Hood*. I still enjoy reading that book and looking at the pictures more than fifty years after I first set eyes on it. I've subsequently read histories

Sherwood Forest is a magical place.

and novels portraying the great outlaw and seen a myriad screen adaptations. In my opinion, neither Kevin Costner nor Russel Crowe hold a candle to Errol Flynn's Robin, although I did get hooked by Michael Praed's *Robin of Sherwood*.

In 2018, Marsha and I entered the pub at the Dukeries Lodge in Edwin-stowe, where we met a local couple who were Facebook friends (and who proved to be delightful company in real life). They offered to walk us through nearby Sherwood Forest, that same woods that had been the setting for countless imaginary adventures over the course of my life. Thankfully, it was after the visitor center was closed and hordes of

This temporary art, made from clay and ferns, portrays a modern-day version of the Green Man.

tourists had departed. As we stepped into the fern-carpeted forest full of ancient oaks I had one of those rare and wonderful moments when you realizes that a real-world place is just as you imagined it would be. It was easy to envision Robin, Friar Tuck, and Marian crouching behind the foliage.

Near the Major Oak—believed to the be the site of the Merry Men's forest encampment—who should I meet but my friend the Green Man. There had just been a local event that encouraged artists to adorn the trunks of these venerable trees with the Green Man's visage rendered in impermanent materials.

In fact, the Sherwood Forest National Nature Reserve has embraced the Green Man. A sign outside the visitors' center features a lovely carving of the Green Man and invites visitors to "follow the Green Man" and "discover the Spirit of Sherwood forest." And there you have it—our leafy friend has become the official patron of Robin's woods! In the visitors' center there is the following explanation:

Robin Hood: A Green Man?

Are Robin Hood and the pagan "Green Man" one and the same? Many people think there may be a connection between Robin Hood and this symbol of rebirth and fertility. The Green Man is a very old pagan (non-Christian) symbol, a mysterious spirit of nature often depicted by medieval wood and stone carvers as a face with leaves sprouting from nose, mouth and eyes. Medieval stone masons added these decorative carvings to churches perhaps in reference to their older, pagan beliefs. In many ways Robin Hood is also a symbol of the old ways and the old religion under which life was better, game was plentiful, and taxes less punishing. In pre-Christian times large old trees like those in Sherwood Forest were regarded as sacred and became the focus of rituals. This is probably how some of our folk traditions like dancing around the May pole started. By the 1500s May Day festivities were commonly called "Robin Hood's Games"—other names

This modern Green Man from a building in Bradwell-on-Sea in England sprouts acanthus leaves like his more ancient brothers. His joyously puckish expression also harkens back to the mischief of Robin Goodfellow.

for the central figure were "Robin-in-the-Hood," "Robin Goodfellow" and "Jack-in-the-Green." Even today, some May Day games still feature the characters of Robin Hood and Maid Marian.

Lady Raglan would be delighted to see how—eighty years after her paper on the Green Man—a national institution follows her assertion that the Green Man is a Pagan Nature deity; apparently the curators haven't been reading more recent scholarship. However, the last paragraph in the Sherwood Forest sign—the connection between Robin Hood and the May Day festivities—is correct. There is substantial overlap between Robin Hood and Jack in the Green. (For those interested to learn more about the connections between the Green Man and the outlaw of Sherwood Forest the book *Robin Hood* by John Matthews offers a thorough and detailed explanation.)

Robin Hood's very name connects him with the ancient tales of faeries: Puck, the mischievous character in *A Midsummer Night's Dream*, is also known as Robin Goodfellow. Puck is called Hob as well, and "Hob," "Hod," and "Hood" are interchangeable in old English. Tales were told of Robin Goodfellow and his merry band of wood sprites leading wild dances through the forests, and these tales may have inspired the May Day revelries.

May Day rites focused on the union of the May King and the May Queen. The May King is sometimes represented by our friend Jack in the Green, but he is also commonly referred to as Robin Hood, and the early tales of the outlaw are woven

The Green Man and his Merry Men

thoroughly into May Day dances and pageants. The May Queen and May King are married in a ceremonial archway called Robin's Bower.

And consider the heroine of the tale, for in every retelling of Robin Hood, his romance with Maid Marian is paramount. The name Marian—diminutive of Mary—is the most common name imaginable in medieval Europe where the Mother of God was venerated on level with her child. Yet there appears to be more going on

Stories about Robin Hood, Maid Marian, and Robin Hood's band of merry men have captured people's imagination for centuries.

with Maid Marian's designation. In the very old May Day revelries, the "Maid," "Marian," and the "May Queen" are interchangeable titles for the Flower Bride. So Robin Hood–Maid Marian and Jack in the Green–the May Queen are transposable pairs of symbolic figures in this ritual that heralds the fertility of each new summer.

If you recall in the earlier chapter titled "What About the Green *Women*?" I visited the amazing Chapter House in Southwell Minster, which is adorned with lifelike stone carvings of thick foliage, and in which I found a face that looks

This production of Shakespeare's A Midsummer Night's Dream *has a Puck (also referred to in the play as Robin Goodfellow) who looks very much like a Green Man.*

like a Green Woman—or an androgynous visage. I wondered if perhaps this face, also known as the Oak King, might not represent a faerie spirit of the forest. The stone carvings in the Chapter House sit above the wooden thrones of the Bishops of the Diocese, each engraved with their title, and one of those reads "Episcopus de Sherwood." I can't help but wonder what connections there might be between the leafy faces in

The Green Man and his Merry Men **133**

"Green Man" pub signs prior to the twentieth century were more likely to portray Robin Hood than the leafy visage of what we today consider to be a Green Man.

Southwell Minster, Robin Goodfellow, and the legendary outlaw of nearby Sherwood Forest.

In the centuries between the High Middle Ages and the early twentieth century, there were dozens of pubs and inns named "The Green Man." Lady Raglan used that phrase to describe both the leaf faces and Jack in the Green, forming our popular modern conception of the Green Man. In recent years the institution of the English pub has declined and some of the Green Man pubs have gone out of business. Those that survive have in most cases redone their signs to reflect popular understanding of the Green Man as a foliated face like those found in old carvings. But the Green Man Pub in Prestwood, Buckinghamshire, is more typical of Green Man pub signs of the past, with its portrayal of the Sherwood Forest outlaw bending his longbow. For patrons of public inns and drinking establishment in Victorian England, the Green Man was Robin Hood.

If we were to attempt a chart showing all the connections between Robin Hood and Jack in the Green, it would soon resemble an appropriate tangle-wood forest. We may never know which came first—the outlaw champion of the poor, Robin Goodfellow the faerie, or Jack in the Green dancing on May Day—but Robin Hood is definitely a branch on the Green Man's family tree. And that Green Man family tree has kept growing and growing, becoming an enormous forest in our modern age.

And now, let's consider another possible family connection for our green friend. This one comes from much farther afield—the Islamic world of the Middle East.

The Green Man and his Merry Men **135**

Al-Khidr's green clothing is said to represent freshness of spirit and eternal liveliness, drawn from the Water of Life. According to tradition, Khidr is the guide of all those who seek spiritual growth and life.

A Wise (Green) Man from the East

You never know where you'll gain a fascinating bit of new information (especially if you're willing to be a bit weird).

In July 2016, I spoke about the Green Man at the Flagstaff, Arizona, Celtic Highland Festival, and I dressed appropriately, with oak leaves in my bonnet and green makeup all over my face. Later in the day, I attended a "stand-up" storytelling workshop where the most impressive story came from a man who had only recently learned of Celtic customs passed down in his racially and culturally blended family. A few minutes after that workshop, I found myself next to the storyteller, waiting in line at the beer tent. He asked, "What's up with your outfit?"

I briefly explained the Green Man, and he exclaimed, "Oh, you mean al-Khidr!" When I confessed my unfamiliarity with the name, he explained, "He's the Green Man," and told about this element of his Muslim faith. My subsequent research revealed there is indeed a proposed link between al-Khidr and the Western Green Man.

According to Islamic tradition, Khidr is an angel or an immortal human messenger or prophet who guards the sea, teaches secret knowledge, aids those in distress, and guides all of us who are on a spiritual journey. His name literally means the "Green One" or "Verdant One." He is a righteous servant of God who possesses great wisdom and mystic knowledge.

Khidr's ancient origins are debated; he may be a descendant of legends from ancient Canaan or Babylon, or possibly related to other legends from Turkey. You may recall that in the chapter on the Green Man's family tree we looked at the foliated head from Al-Hadr,

Al-Khidr is said to unite the opposites in life, bringing growth and creative ingenuity out of destruction.

Iraq, which may also portray an early form of the Khidr tales.

In the Holy Quran, Khidr is not mentioned by name, but he is thought to be the servant of God who meets the Prophet Moses, accompanies him on his travels, does miracles, and teaches Moses that things that appear destructive or unwelcome may—despite first impressions—be blessings. In the Hadith, Mohammad states that the Prophet Elijah meets annually with Khidr in Jerusalem during Ramadan.

Could the Middle Eastern traditions of al-Khidr have influenced the Green Man we see carved in Britain's churches? Cultural links between Islam and Europe during the Middle Ages render the idea plausible. As an example of cultural exchange between medieval East and West, the

The Dome of al-Khidr on the Temple Mount in Jerusalem's Old City is said to be the site of Elijah's annual meeting with Khidr.

A Wise (Green) Man from the East

pointed arch—a signifier of Gothic era church architecture—may be derived from Islamic architecture brought to Europe via returning Crusaders. Templar churches display Palestinian influence and—we shall see in a subsequent chapter—there are Green Men in Knights Templar chapels. The Franciscan friars, hugely influential throughout Europe in the High Middle Ages, maintained a dialogue with their Sufi counterparts from the time of Saint Francis's meeting with Sultan al-Kamil in 1218. Muslim figures appear in Arthurian tales, and some scholars allege that the Green Knight was inspired by contact with Islam. In fact, the Green Knight and al-Khidr may be closely linked.

The color green has deep cross-cultural meaning. It is the

Al-Khidr is associated with fish and the sea. His presence is said to bring green vegetation to desert land (and spiritual growth to seeking hearts).

"fingerprint" or "signature" left on our living world by water and light—and Khidr is connected to both, just as all vegetation is. As the Sufi poet Rumi wrote,

The sign is in the face.
You can look at an orchard
and tell if it rained last night.
That freshness is the sign.

Still, the associations between the Green Man of Eastern tradition and the Green Man of European church decoration is unlikely to be very close, due to their artistic distinctions. Khidr is called "the Green One," but he is never portrayed as having vegetation sprouting from his face or mouth. He may be a saint or illuminated master, but he is not a human-vegetative hybrid.

We need to dig deeper for insight into the soul of the Green Man. In doing so, it may prove helpful to consider where in their churches those medieval artists placed the Green Man's image.

A modern image inspired by the Green Man of Sutton Benger in England, this fellow spews out hawthorn leaves bearing berries. The Celts considered the hawthorn to be a marker between this world and the Other World; the tree often grew beside holy wells. The most famous hawthorn is at Glastonbury; according to legend, Joseph of Arimathea brought it there from the Holy Land. The hawthorn tree's berries—the haws—are beloved by birds, and their inclusion here reminds us of the ways in which all life is interconnected.

The Green Man at the Sacred Threshold

As I've mentioned, my first meeting with a foliated head was inside St. Canice's Cathedral in Kilkenny, and the tour guide—with all good intentions—introduced the Green Man under false pretenses. Here's basically what she told me: "The masons who carved medieval cathedrals held to the old religion, and to the gods of the old religion, but these beliefs were forbidden by the church. So a mason would labor until an entire church edifice was completed. Then, he would sneak back into the church one night, hammer out the visage of the ancient fertility god in a nook of the church, pack up his tools, and leave town before daybreak. Church authorities were thus left with an undesired pagan symbol carved into the recesses of their sanctuary."

Similar explanations have been retold ad nauseum by church docents, on the Internet, and in guide books. It's basically a variation of Lady Raglan's original thesis, in her work that introduced the term "Green Man" into common parlance. You'll recall that she said, "The fact is that unofficial paganism subsisted side by side with the official religion, and this explains the presence of the Green Man." He is, according to Lady Raglan and countless others who followed her lead, a portrayal of a pre-Christian fertility god, a covert Pagan symbol slyly placed in Christian churches. This has been repeated so often that it's rarely contradicted, even though scholars of art and history are now inclined to reject the idea.

Symbols are multivalent, and there are always shades of meaning. As we've already discussed, it's likely that the Green Man's form is influenced by earlier Classical and Celtic art. It's also possible that Jack in the Green who appears in May Day dances may well be a continuation of ancient fertility rites. But there's little reason to believe that the foliated heads carved in churches are quite the same as Jack in the Green who appears in folk dances.

The vegetation-spewing faces in churches are distinctive and indicate a well understood common meaning, agreed upon by artists, clerics, and nobles. I do not believe that the artists who made thousands of Green Men during the Middle Ages intended to convey an "unofficial paganism" with these images, and the places where foliated heads are located in medieval places of worship supports my contention.

Furthermore, medieval Green Man images were not carved in haste. They are usually finely executed, given the same time and attention as surrounding artistic motifs.

This fifteenth-century baptismal font from St. Andrew's Church in Bulmer, Essex, shows a Green Man with grapes and grape leaves erupting from his eyes and mouth. There is nothing furtive about his placement on this central Christian symbol, and the fact that he is flanked by angels further indicates that his creator felt that he belonged in a Christian setting.

The Green Man at the Sacred Threshold

And they are not usually "hidden." Although sometimes they are up high in the corbels, beams, or roof bosses, they are more often placed in obvious and prominent places, and in some cases—such as the "greeter" faces—they are unmissable. If a master carver could chip one of those images beside the front door of a cathedral and not be noticed by the churchmen supervising the work, that would be the greatest miracle ever heard of. Furthermore, many Green Men are placed within a larger aesthetic whole—in other words, they are part of a larger artistic pattern, again indicating that there is nothing covert or hasty in their design.

This thirteenth-century Green Man is placed at the very center of the quire screen in Westminster Abbey, indicating that he was considered central to the church's worship.

But could this be an example of physically obvious images with a hidden meaning? Might this be an inside joke, where the peasants knew that the Green Man was the face of their pre-Christian god, while the clerics just thought it was a pretty bit of art? That might be, except that the Green Man frequently appears in places that are central to the patterns of medieval worship. Since the Green Man is commonly positioned in places of utmost sacred symbolism for medieval Christians, he must symbolize values central to their beliefs.

Bernard of Clairvaux founded the Cistercian order, a tradition that dominated religious life during the high Middle Ages. Bernard opposed fantastical images in church buildings "which attract the worshipper's gaze and hinder his attention." The Cistercians were known for their deep

This serene-looking Green Man can be found in Dore Abbey, where his visage must have inspired the Cistercian monks who worshipped there.

A Green Man in Melrose Abbey.

and simple piety, and if a Cistercian monastic house contained art, that art clearly portrayed Christian beliefs. So, it's worthy of note that there is a cherubic-looking Green Man in the Cloister of Cistercian Dore Abbey, Herefordshire. Bernard's disciples must have seen something edifying in

The Green Man at the Sacred Threshold

that carved face. Green Men also appear at Melrose Abbey, another Cistercian monastery

For another example of the Green Man as a symbol integral to medieval Christianity, consider its appearance on baptismal founts. The baptismal fount at Brecon Cathedral, Wales, which we've already discussed, is almost a thousand years old and has been used to christen untold generations of children into salvation, according to the belief of those who observe this rite. Around the fount are symbols of the four Gospels and—connecting them—prominent faces of four Green Men.

This Green Man drawing, based on a baptismal font in St. John's Church in Coolbanagher, Ireland, is wearing a bishop's mitre, indicating that he is clearly a Christian symbol. The vine the spews out of his mouth encircles the entire font, enclosing within its embrace three angels.

I found further reinforcement for my belief about the Green Man being a Christian symbol at St. Winifred's Church in Branscombe, Devon. Branscombe is a lovely seaside village tucked away on England's southern coast, and the village even includes a working medieval blacksmith shop. Marsha and I have been privileged to stay on several occasions in a sprawling house with parts dating to before the Norman Conquest, and crenellations from the time when they were intended to keep intruders out. The house is also said to be haunted, and the former owner was a famous writer on topics paranormal. Alas, despite best efforts, I've not encountered a ghost in that ancient Branscombe house. But I did find a Green Man at an interesting place in the local parish church.

St. Winifred's Church is a history lesson in stone, with bits dating to Saxon, Viking, Norman, and Tudor eras. As I walked inside, I found myself beside a big medieval baptismal font, ornamented with two protruding Green Men.

Baptism is one of the most important sacraments observed in all Christian denominations; it signifies the entrance of believers into the Church, which makes the baptismal font a portal to the life of faith. For this reason, medieval baptismal fonts are decorated with appropriate images, such as the signs of the four Gospels, the Apostles, grapevines (a symbol of life-in-Christ expressed by Jesus in the Gospels), Christ's resurrection, and so on. Given the Green Man's presence on baptismal fonts, it stands to reason that the Green Man is a symbol that fits beside other symbols of spiritual rebirth and the Christian faith.

You also see the Green Man on medieval rood screens, the elaborately carved partitions that separate the chancel (used only by priests to celebrate the Mass)

The St. Winifred baptistry is yet another example of a Green Man playing a role in the sacred sacrament of baptism.

from the nave (used by common people). This was a most holy threshold in medieval churches, representing the curtain to the Holy of Holies in the Jerusalem temple, the boundary between what is sacred and what is profane. It would be the last place for an image that didn't represent the Christian faith.

On a brief stop in the Church of St. Michael in Chagford, Devon, I was drawn to the amazing carvings that cover the rood screen, a rare survivor from rot and insects, that dates back to medieval times. I grinned as I spotted a Green Man. And then I saw another, and another, and . . . Ultimately, I counted eight different Green Men prominently carved on the front of the screen. The Eucharist, the rite believed to ensure each worshiper's participation in God's salvation, was served at the rood screen.

We've looked at two areas of medieval church architecture—the baptismal font and the rood screen—where the rites central to Christian religion were celebrated, and we have noted that they are decorated with foliated heads. The Green Man was not a representation of unofficial Paganism: rather, he appears at those places that symbolize entrance into the Christian faith (baptism) and then assurance of continuity in that faith (the Eucharist). Both baptism and Eucharist are metaphorical thresholds of faith; they symbolize transition into the Christ-life.

Are there other examples of the Green Man placed at the portals of religious belief? Yes. In fact, a great many. Remember the "greeter" Green Man at Dornoch Cathedral, and at Kilpeck Church? The door into the church was obviously and literally entrance into sacred space. Coming to church (often daily) for celebration of the Mass was a vital part of religious

Green Men on rood screens (from top to bottom): the Church of St. Nicholas in Blakeney, Norfolk; the Church of St. Michael in Chagford, Devon; St. Michael's Church in Mere, Wiltshire; and Cartmel Priory, Cumbria.

Taken from a Green Man on the sixteenth-century rood screen in the church in Marwood, Devon, England. The custom of screening off the altar—where the rood, or crucifix, was placed—is very ancient. It emphasized the sacred mystery surrounding the place of sacrifice (possibly a survival of Judaism, to which the Celtic Christians felt particularly close). For the Green Man to be placed here indicates the connection between this image and the medieval understanding of Christ.

life in the Middle Ages—and here again, we find the Green Man positioned at a sacred portal.

I've been building a case that the foliated faces in worship spaces must represent an idea integral to medieval Christian faith. This is proven by Green Men carved carefully at places of baptism, communion, and entrance to the sanctuary. But what about those Green Men—like the one in Saint Canice's Cathedral—that are put in high places, such as corbels, the tops of pillars, ceiling bosses or rafters? Were these indeed placed to be hidden—or do they too serve some sort of "threshold" function?

For thousands of years the abode of God and the angels

was thought to be "upward" from the earth. We moderns have more sophisticated notions of the heavenly realm as a "parallel dimension," perhaps more slantwise than upward, but for people in the Middle Ages, upward meant God-ward. The ceiling of a church, along with its supporting apparatus, was a symbolic threshold to the Divine realm.

The Green Man was consistently rendered in places that represent portals of faith—places of rebirth and communion with God—in medieval churches. This is an important clue to his identity. Let's continue to turn over the leaves of history, seeking the Green Man's deeper nature, as we look at Green Men associated with the legend-shrouded order of the Knights Templar.

A Green Man taken from the ceiling of the cloisters of Durham Cathedral.

The Green Man at the Sacred Threshold **153**

One of the Green Men of Rosslyn Chapel.

In the Temples of the Warrior Monks

13

On a lovely May day in rural Herefordshire, Marsha and I stepped out of our rental car, walked past a stately yew, and approached the compact fortress-like structure of St. Michael's Church, Garway, in Herefordshire, a small church with a unique history. I was particularly interested in the mysterious, foreboding Green Man that I'd heard made his home here.

St. Michael's Church in Garway is historically linked with the legendary Order of the Knights Templar. There are only a few bona fide Templar churches still intact in the UK, and Garway is one of those. In recent years the Templars have entered popular culture in the popular *Da Vinci Code* by Dan Brown, and they are the subject of the onscreen fantasy series *Knightfall*. The Templars have been the subject of centuries of speculations, having to do with the Holy Grail, a lost treasure, the Shroud of Turin, and even an alleged expedition to the New World predating Columbus.

Even in their own time, the Templars inspired tall tales. Despite the pervasive violence of the Middle Ages, people still had some understanding that God does not desire violence; at the end of life, medieval warriors felt the need to be absolved of the killing they'd done. The Templars, who combined the competing values of warfare and religion, inspired the public imagination. They gave more ordinary warriors hope for the salvation of their souls.

The official name of the order was "The Poor Knights of the Temple of Solomon," since they undertook the monastic vow of poverty.

St. Michael's Church in Garway. The earliest record of a monastery on the site is in the seventh century, but most of the current church was built in the twelfth and thirteenth centuries, including the massive defensible tower, which was once separate from the main church building.

The Templars were founded in 1119 and grew rapidly in membership and power. Templar knights, in their distinctive white mantles with a red cross, were among the most skilled fighting units of Crusades, but most of the members of the order were actually non-combatants who managed a vast economic infrastructure throughout Christendom, developing innovative financial techniques that were an early form of banking. In effect, they formed the world's first multinational corporation. They were closely tied to the Crusades, and when the Holy Land was lost, support for the order faded. Rumors about the Templars' secret ceremonies created distrust, and King Philip of France, who was deeply in debt to the order, took advantage of this to destroy them and erase his debt. In 1307, he had many of the order's members arrested, tortured into giving false confessions, and burned at the stake. Pope Clement disbanded the order in 1312 under pressure from King Philip.

In the Temples of the Warrior Monks

Entrusted with banking for Crusaders and pilgrims in the Holy Land, they ironically became incredibly wealthy, which led to the jealousy of monarchs and church leaders—and eventually, to their demise.

Their headquarters was the Temple Mount in Jerusalem, the site of fabled King Solomon and of the Ark of the Covenant, and that added to the Templars' legendary mystique. The Grail Knights of Arthurian legend are much like the Templars, and the Holy Grail was associated with the Templars' Jerusalem center.

The destruction of the Templar order in 1307 also led to a flurry of rumors; under the horrors of torture, Templars confessed to heresy, including the worship of "Baphomet," a heathen idol. Most historians assume that this was a name conveniently planted by torturers, to ensure it came out of the screaming mouths of their victims, but there has been endless speculation over the past seven centuries about what "Baphomet" could be. Some say it was a skull . . . or a three-headed Pagan idol . . . or the devil . . . or—more positively—the Shroud of Turin, or even the Holy Grail.

And "Baphomet" has also been suggested as an explanation for the sinister-looking Green Man situated on the outside of the chancel archway in the Garway Church.

In the twelfth century, 2,000 acres in Garway were given to the Knights Templar. They built the church there and farmed the land to raise funds for their brethren in the Holy Land. The church was built for fortification as well as worship, as these were Norman knights on the contested Welsh Border.

Fascinating details of the church connect it with the Templars, including a circular ruined nave that was built to imitate Solomon's Temple. The outside of the church is carved with symbols that include a Jerusalem Cross, a Templar Cross, a dragon, the hand of God, and others. In the floor of the church are Templar gravestones, and a sign in the side chapel says, "In this chapel the Templars were installed into their order."

And there is the so-called Green Man. Before I set foot in Herefordshire, my thoughts about this image were influenced by a novel in one of my favorite detective series, the Merrily Watkins mysteries by author Phil Rickman. Merrily is a Church of England priest tasked with ghost-busting for the church. In the novel *The Fabric of Sin*, a Garway Green Man is associated with sinister manifestations (although in the novel, Rickman moved the Green Man outside the church, to a nearby building).

Is there a dark secret hidden in the soul of this Green Man? His gaze made me feel uncomfort-

This horned figure, commonly identified as the Garway Green Man, has been used to prove the Pagan roots of the Green Man. Some authors have gone so far as to say that it indicates that the Green Man had diabolic roots as well.

An image on a nineteenth-century bellows, indicating the durability of this image from the Middle Ages through the centuries. The horns on this one imply a connection to the demonic in the nineteenth-century mind. Alternatively, in the Vulgate version of the Bible in Exodus 34, it speaks of Moses coming down from Mount Sinai with horns on his head. This does not mean that he had been communicating with the devil, but that the horns were evidence of sacred power and authority.

able. Most Green Men cheer me up when I'm gazing at them, but this one gave me the shivers.

Signage in the church says this face is "an unusual head with beaded decoration that gives rise to much speculation." And the official church guidebook says it is "a superb head and many explanations are offered as to its identification." Notice that neither official document refers to it as a "Green Man." And, having stared at it a good while, I don't think it is a Green Man.

Here's my take: the Garway "Green Man" appears on the outside of the entrance to the church's chancel, separating the area around the altar from the more mundane space within the church. As you look at the image on page 159, note that instead of leaves coming out of the mouth, there appears to be a cord—complete with tassels—wrapped around the face. If there's no foliage, it's not a Green Man. The Garway church is dedicated to Saint Michael the Archangel, who in the

After the dissolution of the Templars, the Church of St. Michael's in Garway was given to the Order of Knights of Saint John of Jerusalem, a monastic and military order tasked with providing hospitality for pilgrims to the Holy Land. They provided care for rich, for poor, for Christians and—note this, in a world divided by religious prejudice— for Muslims. This religious order cared for the Garway Church until the Protestant Reformation.

Book of Revelation binds Satan—and I believe that is what this face portrays: it is an image of Satan who has been bound by the church's patron, the angel Michael, and who is therefore prevented from having influence within the inner sanctum of this sacred space. That would accord well with the symbolism and thinking of the Templars.

Rosslyn Chapel was built in the fifteenth century, and has been in the care of the St. Clair family for six centuries. Architecturally and artistically, it is a unique tour-de-force.

The interior of Rosslyn Chapel is filled with ornate and intricate stonework. It's as if a faerie forest has grown all over the sanctuary, a celebration of the Celtic and natural spiritual worlds.

There is another church associated with both the Templars and the Green Man, and that is the famous Rosslyn Chapel, officially named the Collegiate Chapel of St. Matthew, which is located about a half hour south of Edinburgh, Scotland.

Like many other readers, I knew of Rosslyn Chapel because of *The Da Vinci Code*; it features prominently in the book, and it was used as a filming location for the movie. I was curious to see this famous site—and it more than lived up to its reputation. Stepping inside the sanctuary took my breath away. The interior is filled, top-to-bottom and side-to-side, with realistic, finely executed carving. Everything you could imagine in the medieval mythic and natural realm appears here.

Rosslyn Chapel has definite Templar associations, despite being con-

Here are just three of the more than a hundred Green Men that inhabit Rosslyn Chapel. (Note that the center one appears to be a skull with grape vines growing out of the mouth and eyes. This is symbolism we will discuss further in a later chapter.)

structed after the dissolution of the Templar order. There is ample documentation showing that members of the order found refuge and continued their vocations in Scotland after they were persecuted in England. (For those interested in this topic I recommend *The Knights Templar and Scotland* by Robert Ferguson.) The St. Clair family, who built Rosslyn Chapel, were important in the Templar Order, and there are numerous artistic details in the church that indicate Templar connections.

And it is the forest of the Green Man! In the stone tangle-wood of Rosslyn Chapel, there are more than a hundred Green Men; no other church has so many Green Men per square foot. Photography is prohibited in the chapel, so you won't see many of these online or in print, but he appears here in full artistic splendor, each face a distinct individual, some appearing beneficent, others puckish, and a few forbidding. The offi-

Drawings based on two more of Rosslyn Chapel's Green Men.

cial guide states, "The Green Man symbolized the capacity for great goodness and the parallel scope for significant evil," which I think is a good summation of the tribe of the Green Man in Rosslyn Chapel.

The Green Man's ambivalent nature, seen in these temples of the warrior monks, raises a point worth pondering: can we assume that the soul of the Green Man is kindly? Were these foliated heads perhaps harbingers of warning or condemnation? It's a question worthy of our next chapter.

This Green Man is taken from the church of St Andrew, Sampford Courtenay, Devon, where it is a ceiling boss above the altar.

All Flesh Is Grass

Before we visited Orkney in 2016, we'd been on multiple trips to the Scottish Highlands and Border region, since Scotland is the land of my family heritage. We had ideas of what to expect from travels in Scotland—but then we discovered that Orkney is different. Orcadians talk about "Scotland" as another country! There are as many Norwegian flags flying there as Scotland's Saltire flag, and the accents are entirely different. All this betrays the fact that Orkney was settled and ruled by the Vikings for much of its history.

St. Magnus Cathedral in Kirkwall offers a rare opportunity—the chance to visit a Viking church, while still in the UK. The cathedral is an enormous edifice of dark reddish stone, dominating the skyline of one of the island's main cities. The entrance is a glorious Romanesque arch of multi-colored hues.

I strolled through the interior of the cathedral, past cyclopean columns, noting a Templar cross carved into the wall. Then I came to a display with illustrations of the life of Saint Magnus, the cathedral's patron saint. His story proved to be a real contrast to the warrior monks of the Templar order.

Magnus converted to Christ and got the message that Jesus didn't want him to kill people. He sat through a bloody sea battle reciting psalms from the prow of a longboat, refusing to take life. Later, when confronted by his enemies, he again refused to take up the sword and was martyred. So there I was in Scotland, in a church made by Vikings, celebrating a Viking who was a pacifist.

Construction of St. Magnus Cathedral began in 1137, when the island was ruled by the Norse Earls, and it was added to over the next three hundred years. It was named for the martyred uncle of one of the Earls. Magnus had a reputation for piety and gentleness, refusing to fight when his kinfolk went raiding. According to tradition, Magnus was killed in a family feud when his cousin's cook hit him over the head with an axe.

The interior of St. Magnus. In 1917, a hidden cavity in one of the columns was discovered. Inside, was a box with bones including a skull showing a wound consistent with a blow from an axe. Could these be the remains of Saint Magnus? No one knows for sure.

I had to ask a guide to find a Green Man. There's one on a column near the front of the church, crudely carved, a rather sad-looking fellow, I thought, who appears to be vomiting a string of vegetation out of his mouth. Later, I noticed two other foliated faces photographed in the cathedral guidebook (I'd failed to notice them in the actual building), with this description: "Originally a fertility symbol, it was used to represent corruption of the flesh, the leaves representing sin and decay."

That's certainly a dour take on the Green Man, but others have voiced similar thoughts. Richard Hayman, architectural historian and author of the Shire Library Green Man book, refers to ninth-century theologian Rabanus Maurus who "described leaves as representing lust and sins of the flesh." He also refers to the medieval depictions of vines and leaves as a "tanglewood . . . a metaphor for the human condition," insofar as forest wilderness "trapped men physically" and also "impeded them morally."

All the Flesh Is Grass

Historically, vines, both artistically and linguistically, are more likely to represent life and union with Jesus, but a Bible reference does use vegetation as symbolic of life's ephemeral nature: "All people are like grass, and all their glory is like the flowers of the field; the grass withers and the flowers fall" (1 Peter 1:24 NIV).

This image is based on on a grave slab that dates back to the tenth or eleventh century. The slab has been attributed to the shrine of Saint Ragenor, an Anglo-Saxon prince who was slain by the Vikings in 870. His grave had been forgotten until the visions of an elderly man drew a priest to the burial site. Many miracles were said to have been wrought at the grave and the king (Edward the Confessor) had a great shrine erected for him. The Green Man's trailing foliage entwines within a number of beasts, including a cat and a dog.

So is the Green Man a reminder of mortality and life's fleeting nature? Maybe. The Green Man's image doesn't only appear in churches; he also populates cemeteries, indicating that the Green Man was associated with death. Often the graveyard Green Man is portrayed as an empty skull exploding with greenery.

In the Middle Ages, people were far more familiar with the concept of death than we are today. Life spans were short, most children died before they reached their fifth birthday, and death was a regular visitor to all families, rich and poor. The great plague that decimated Europe in the middle of the fourteenth century wiped out populations and reduced society to chaos. Medieval artists, reflecting the world in which they lived and its concerns, often portrayed death on the walls of churches. Over the centuries,

One of the Green Men in St. Magnus Cathedral. These leaves may symbolize sin and decay, but there could also be a far more positive side to this image: the leaves might represent new life taking root out of decay and death (as is true in the natural world). The expression on this Green Man's face indicates the process he's undergoing is not altogether pleasant, a reminder that flesh is mortal—and yet look at that healthy, fully leaved, almost muscular vine springing out of his mouth!

All the Flesh Is Grass

The Green Man's image is often found in cemeteries as well as churches, indicating that he symbolized both death and the promise of new life. This image is taken from a gravestone found in Shebbear, Devon.

A drawing of an 18th-century gravestone in Edinburgh, Scotland, shows the Green Man's supremacy over the skull-and-crossbones of death.

most of these have faded and been painted over, but a few remain. A common motif is "the dance of death," skeletal reminders of mortality.

Certainly, the soul of the Green Man includes the reality of death. The Green Man is a symbol of transformation, and death is a necessary element in any process of change. As Jesus said in John's Gospel, "Very truly I tell you, unless a kernel of wheat falls to the ground and dies, it remains only a single seed. But if it dies, it produces many seeds" (John 12:24 NIV).

Medieval thought included death as an element contained within all spheres of reality—a more realistic view than modern attempts to sanitize mortality—but the medieval view of Nature was more broadly life affirming. Greenery generally represented not decay but *veriditas*, the power within all living things to replenish, renew, heal, and restore.

As I looked at the Green Man in the immense Norse cathedral in Orkney, I came to a realization: he may be in the process of death and decay—but he's spitting out new life.

I have a hidden meaning. I was portrayed in a thousand different ways in the past, and I keep sprouting again in the twenty-first century. Don't you want to know who I am? (Thirteenth-century Green Man from Bamberg, Germany, with a face composed entirely of acanthus leaves,)

The Myth Behind the Face

By now you've armchair-traveled with me through old stone churches, through history from Roman times to the early twentieth century, and through legend from the Islamic Middle East to Arthurian Romance, searching for the soul of the Green Man. I've concluded that the Green Men in medieval churches probably were not intended to portray a specific Pagan deity, nor Al-Khadir the Muslim sage, nor Gawain's Green Knight. On the side of positive identifications, the Green Man is one inhabitant of the God-infused medieval world, appears in places that symbolized salvation and rebirth, and conveyed something valuable for Christians in the Middle Ages.

So, what *did* these foliated heads found in churches throughout Europe mean to the medieval people who commissioned and carved them? The most convincing explanation that I've found of the Green Man's meaning comes from Oxford writer Tim Healey in an article in the *Glasgow Evening Times,* and also from a more detailed account in *The Green Man Unmasked: A New Interpretation of an Ancient Riddle* by James Coulter.

The foundation of this theory is based on a book titled *The Golden Legend*, a hugely popular collection of Christian tales penned in the thirteenth century (although most of these stories existed in oral tradition before then). *The Golden Legend* was so popular in medieval Europe that a thousand handwritten manuscripts still exist. Contained in this text is the tale of Adam and the Tree of Life. This fable is a sequel to the story contained in Hebrew and Christian Bibles, in Genesis chapter 3. In the Bible's account, God creates Paradise and sets Adam and Eve in the presence of two trees: one is the Tree of the Knowledge of Good and Evil and the other is the Tree of Life. When Adam and Eve are seduced by the serpent to eat of the first tree, God expels them from Paradise. *The Golden Legend* includes a follow-up to the account, a fable that tells of the end of Adam's life:

> *And in the end of his life when he should die, it is said, but of none authority, that he sent Seth his son into Paradise for to fetch the oil of mercy, where he received certain grains of the fruit of the tree of mercy by an angel. And when he came again he found his father Adam yet alive and told him what he had done. And then Adam laughed first and then died. And then Seth laid the grains*

or kernels under his father's tongue and buried him in the vale of Hebron; and out of his mouth grew three trees of the three grains, of which trees the cross that our Lord suffered his passion on was made, by virtue of which he gat very mercy, and was brought out of darkness into very light of heaven.

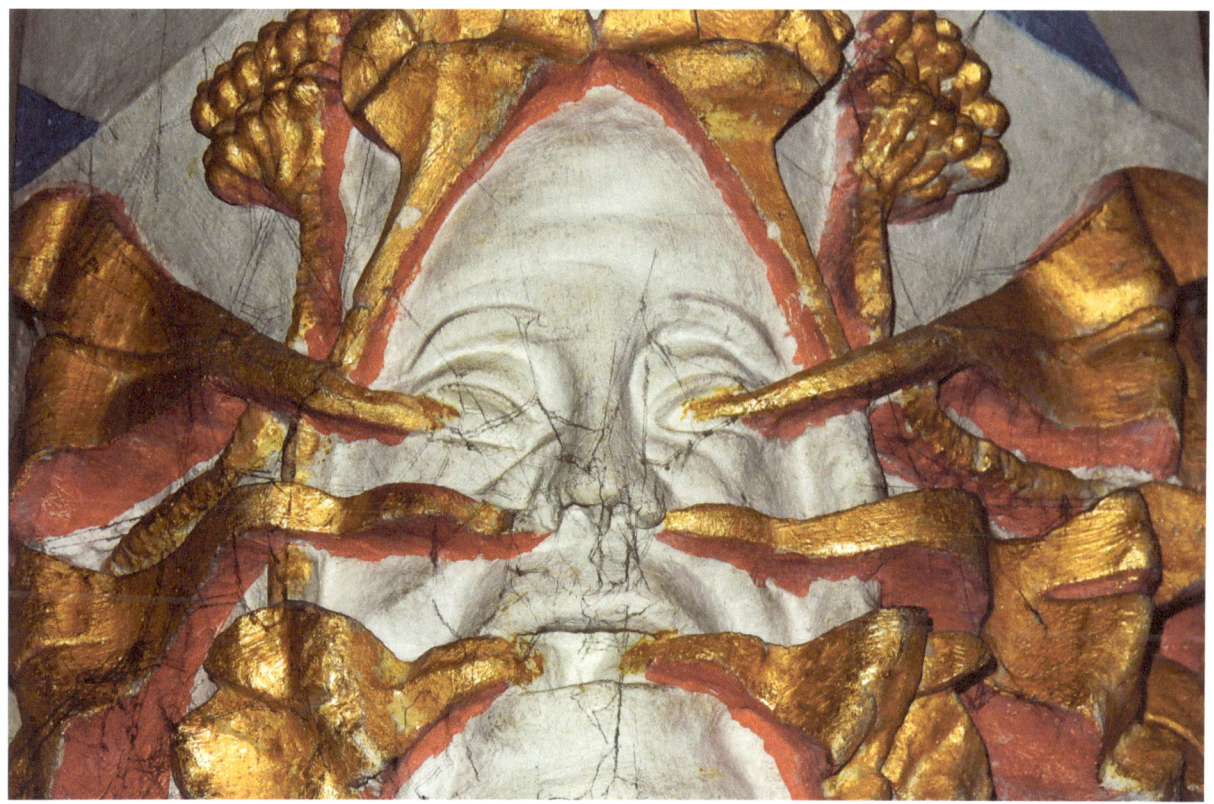

The Green Man in the Lady Chapel of Ottery St. Mary is both gruesome and hopeful. Out of death and corruption springs new gold and glowing life. Note the red paint, as well as gold, perhaps indicating the blood shed at death.

Tim Healey, asks, "Is it possible that this specifically Christian story was in the minds of some, at least, of the mediaeval craftsmen as they fashioned their haunting images?"

I think so, and I see confirmation in the Green Men of my acquaintance. One is found in a prominent position of the Lady Chapel in the Church of Saint Mary, Ottery, Devon. The monks used this chapel for more intimate services than those held for laypeople in the larger area of the church. This Green Man appears to be a death mask, with three strands of brightly painted vegetation growing from his pale face. That fits perfectly with the three trees growing from the face of the deceased Adam in *The Golden Legend*. Other medieval Green Men express similar deathly visages.

Drawn from a carving from the end of a pew in St. Mary's Church, Bishops Lydeard, Somerset, England. The foliage coming from the Green Man's mouth is the Tree of Life growing from the tongue of Adam. Notice the closed eyes, as if the Green Man is sleeping, symbolic of Adam's death. In the Middle Ages death was most often portrayed in Bible terms as "sleep."

Another acanthus-leaf Green Man, this one from the crypt in Canterbury Cathedral, created in 1350.

And then there are the acanthus leaves, which are the most common leaves to surround the Green Man's head. In the ancient world, as we mentioned at the beginning of this books, acanthus symbolized the triumph of life over death. The leaves were often included as architectural features in cemeteries and grave memorials, a comforting visual message indicating immortality. Early Christians appropriated the

A Green Man from a misericord in St. Peter's Church in Wintringham, Yorkshire, England.

motif, and for them, acanthus leaves became a potent visual prophecy of transformation, renewal, and resurrection. This confirms that Green Man images were meant to connect the physical and spiritual death that was Adam's legacy to humanity with the eternal life offered by Christ.

In the Middle Ages, people loved the tales in *The Golden Legend* and considered them part of their faith as much as stories from the Bible. The tale of the Tree of Life sprouting from Adam's mouth reverses the negativity of original sin; the first sinner becomes a means of redemption and thus all human failings may grow into betterment, in league with Nature.

This painting from the Book of Hours of Catherine of Cleves, created in the fifteenth century, shows Seth planting a branch of the Tree of Life in Adam's mouth.

If the Green Man is Adam, then he is also all of us. The Hebrew word *adam* used in the Biblical creation stories is not only a proper noun but is also the word for "humanity," as in Genesis 1:27: "So God created humankind in God's image, in the

The Myth Behind the Face **181**

This image based on a French Green Man carved under a misericord bench in the Abbey in Vendome, completed in 1040, has both oak leaves and acorns, with the acorns signifying the promise of new life. In the eleventh century, during the Norman Conquest, the English carried acorns in their pockets as an emblem of spiritual power and growth. According to an ancient English superstition, if you carried an acorn in your pocket, your youth would be continually renewed.

image of God they were created; male and female God created them," where "humankind" translates the Hebrew word *adam*.

Medieval Christians were well familiar with Saint Augustine of Hippo's famous expression *felix culpa* (Latin for "fortunate sin"). This was the concept that Adam's sin was a blessing (fortunate) for humanity. The tale of the Tree of Life sprouting from Adam's mouth reverses the downward path of humanity; the mouth of the first sinner becomes the soil of redemption, and thus all human failings may grow into a renewed future, in accord with the ways of the natural world. The foliated head—portrayal of the tree of life growing from Adam's visage—was a visual portrayal of *felix culpa*.

Given this significance, we can understand why the Green Man appears on the sacred thresholds in so many medieval places of worship. The image of the Tree of Life sprouting from Adam's mouth would be appropriate for rituals of baptism and communion. It also explains why the Green Man found in churches is almost always a *man*, representing the typical medieval understanding of Adam.

The revision of the story of Adam's apparent "fall" told in *The Golden Legend* suggests that when we bungle things in the worst way, the seeds of an improved future may grow out of those same mistakes. Each of us, in our individual lives, have times when something good emerged from our debacles. And taking this insight into the twenty-first century, we are faced with this new challenge: can we nurture seeds of a healthy life for Planet Earth from the terrible scars we have inflicted on her?

What is the Green Man's secret? *Peer into his eyes and see the soul of Adam, who represents all of humanity. Be comforted and challenged by the glimmer of hope as his death transforms into the greening of a renewed future.*

Inspired by a modern-day carving on a garden wall, this Green Man contains multiple meaningful images from Nature: first, acanthus leaves, with their connection to renewal and life's power to endure beyond death; second, a bird, which in many cultures represents the immortal soul; and finally, the eggs, an ancient symbol of resurrection and new life.

The Perennial Green Man

I expect to run into my friend the Green Man when poking about in old churches; it's a surprise, however, to bump into him at a rave-like party with flashing lights and thumping music.

In 2015, Marsha and I attended the Parliament of World Religions in Salt Lake City, Utah, an event that brought ten thousand people from seventy nations together to share in a vast multifaith discussion of the world's pressing issues. At that event, Episcopal Priest Matthew Fox (known for his works on creation spirituality) conducted a "Cosmic Mass" celebrating the struggles and survival of the Earth. At the end of that, amid pulsing lights and the beat of computer-generated electronic music, a figure on stilts appeared wearing an enormous Green Man mask—the Green Man had leapt from the ancient Morris dances into a thoroughly modern celebration. It was another sign that in the twenty-first century, the Green Man has been liberated from the confines of history to bloom anew.

How did the Green Man survive, from the Middle Ages until now? Many elements of medieval church art were banished in the Reformation era that followed the Middle Ages, but the Green Man continued on. The Protestants who followed the way of Luther and Calvin in the sixteenth and seventeenth centuries could be ruthless in their attempts to eradicate the rival Roman Catholic faith, blowing up abbeys, smashing statues in churches, and killing priests. Christian Europe descended into bloody religious wars. But the leaf-face motif—already centuries old at the time—fared well through this

Notice that this thoroughly modern Green Man, who made his appearance at the 2015 Parliament of World Religions, has an out-thrust tongue, like several of the ancient Green Men we've encountered in this book.

The title page of Luther's Appeal to the General Council, *1520, shows our leafy friend as an integral part of the design.*

unfortunate phase of religious history.

Martin Luther, the German priest who began the Protestant Reformation, may be one reason the Green Man lasted through this time of spiritual upheaval. The newly invented printing press stamped out thousands of copies of Luther's essays, fanning the sparks of Protestantism into flame, and some of those vital documents included illustrations of the Green Man—big and bold, right on the title page.

Luther wrote and spoke about matters he called *adiaphora*—a word meaning "indifferent things." Adiaphora were things "unessential for salvation" and yet meaningful,

The Perennial Green Man

such as stories of the saints, church music, or ecclesiastical art. He compared fellow Reformers to a drunk person who falls off one side of a horse, is righted again, then falls off the other side, symbolizing those who had formerly been addicted to non-biblical traditions, but who now wished to discard such ideas in their entirety. We do not know for certainty, but it fits with Luther's understanding that he would not object to the popular tale of the Tree of Life emerging from Adam's mouth, the legend behind the leaf faces in medieval churches. Luther wrote, "The power of God

This painting of Luther preaching, painted by Lucas Cranach in the sixteenth century, was intended to portray symbolic meaning about Luther's approach to theology, and each detail was chosen to help convey this meaning. Note that Luther is pointing to Jesus, as the Bible lies open before him and he stands in a pulpit that bears the profile of a leafy being. The implication here is that both Nature and the Bible point to Jesus, and this was the message Luther conveyed to his congregation of men, women, and children.

is present at all places, even in the tiniest tree leaf. Do you think God is sleeping on a pillow in heaven? . . . God is wholly present in all creation, in every corner, behind you and before you."

Have you noticed how any item that goes out of popularity—if you hold onto it long enough—will come back again? I count myself fortunate to have bow ties, fountain pens, and vinyl records which were originally prized, then laughably unfashionable, and now have become "hip" again. In a similar manner, the Green Man lived on through the 1600s and 1700s.

A foliated woman at Traquair House in Scotland, painted on a drawing room ceiling between 1500 and 1600, shows how the leaf face motif branched out into more daring—even erotic—interpretations as it transmuted from sacred to household settings. The ill-fated Mary Queen of Scots stayed at Traquair House her last night in Scotland before entering England and being arrested, and then eventually beheaded. I like to think this leafy image might have given her a little smile on such a sad stay.

The Perennial Green Man

Artists of the European Renaissance sought to revive the arts of Classical antiquity, which included images similar to the Green Man. The original of this image was created in the early sixteenth century by Michelangelo. It shows a Green Man with wings on his head, like those of the god Mercury. Mercury was the god of the market, the fleet-footed messenger god. Wings in general indicated a symbolic connection with the Other World, so from this perspective, this image combines Nature, the world of business, and the heavenly. Mercury also had deep significance in alchemy, and Michelangelo is known for embedding alchemical symbols in his work. From an alchemical perspective, Mercury contained many opposites within himself. He contains the four Classical elements: earth, wind, water, fire. In his air aspect, he is the spirit—the wind—that is present everywhere in Nature and brings it to life. As a hermaphrodite, he unifies the sexes within himself. He is both a helper and a trickster; he is bride and groom; alpha and omega, the beginning and the end. He's depicted as both a young man and an old man (as he appears in this Green Man). His association with the Green Man is appropriate, since the Green Man is also a creature of contradiction. He too is the trickster who turns everything on its head and uses paradox to point us beyond the boundaries we've imposed on our ideas about the world.

The inspiration for this Green Man comes from a walnut carving on the end of a pew in Northington, England, created in the late nineteenth century as part of the Victorian Gothic revival. The other pews in the church include carvings of the Four Evangelists, while the Twelve Apostles are portrayed in the church's stained glass, so the Green Man is in good company with the central figures of Christianity, just as his medieval ancestors were.

Perhaps the Green Man lacked the same vitality as he displayed in the Norman era, but he was still smiling and bearing fresh leaves, waiting for his chance to become popular once more.

During the Tudor era in England the Green Man did have to relocate. His favorite places in churches declined in their importance as Protestants changed focus from sacraments (baptism and Eucharist) to the centrality of the spoken word. At the same time, the sorts of ornamentation that were popular in churches during the Middle Ages moved indoors.

Hunkering down indoors, the Green Man survived into the nineteenth century when he flowered again during the Victorian age. Novelists like Sir Walter Scott renewed

The Perennial Green Man

popular interest in the Middle Ages; dusty old Gothic buildings and rusty suits of armor were suddenly deemed "romantic" and in great demand with collectors. Architects began building homes and churches in "Neo-Gothic" style, a trend that would last more than a century. Scott's Abbotsford House was one of the first examples of this revived medieval fashion, and its interior included several Green Men. At the same time, churches that had been allowed to deteriorate since the Reformation were valued again, and many were restored with Gothic flourishes more opulent than the original fittings. This Victorian restoring of medieval artistic forms enabled the Green Man to return to his ancient abodes on church walls and furnishings.

This early twentieth-century leaf face, with both acanthus leaves and grapes, adorns the Crown and Mitre Hotel in Carlisle, England.

In the late nineteenth century, artists and architects such as William Morris popularized the Arts and Crafts Movement which emphasized the purity and quality of pre-industrial workmanship, reviving and combining medieval motifs to create new forms of beauty. This movement was influential on both sides of the Atlantic, and decorated both secular and sacred buildings. At the same time, the Industrial Revo-

Contemporary artistic renderings of the Green Man transcend the ambitions of medieval artists. This image of the Green Man at the Custard Factory in Birmingham, England, erected in 2001 by sculptor Tawney Gray, is 14 meters high.

lution was coming into full steam with the nascent technologies of electricity and carbon fuels, resulting in the rapid expansion—both outward and upward—of great cities and public works. The Green Man benefited from this, flowering both in the abundance and quality of his appearance.

The Green Man struggled through the 1600s and 1700s, bloomed again in the Victorian era, and today, he is sprouting up all over! If numbers are any indication, the twenty-first century is the Green Man's greatest harvest. Just scan Etsy or eBay for Green Man merchandise; you will find pages of plaques, T-shirts, bags, wall coverings, rugs, and other items. No one had ever written about the Green Man until Lady Raglan in the 1930s, yet today there are printed and e-reader books, websites, and coloring books. I have a Green Man bottle opener in the kitchen. While his historical meaning is still a mystery to most

The Perennial Green Man

people, the Green Man clearly resonates with a great many people in our time.

Contemporary creations such as this one reflect our culture's fascination with the concept of human-tree hybrids.

The Green Man also appears in the most popular contemporary format for storytelling—the screen. Any fan of J.R.R. Tolkien's *Lord of the Rings* will immediately think of Tree Beard and his fellow Ents. *Guardians of the Galaxy* and other Marvel films include Groot, the protective companion of his superhero friends. The *Harry Potter* films feature the screaming and very anthropomorphic Mandrake roots, and the offshoot series *Fantastic Beasts and Where to Find Them* includes the diminutive human-tree hybrids called bowtruckles. The movie *A Wrinkle in Time* makes a significant change from the novel regarding Mrs. Whatsit's non-human form; in the book she becomes a winged horse, but, in the movie, she changes into a winged being with a Classical foliated head.

In recent decades the Green Man has also taken his place in celebrations of spirituality and environmentalism. Partly this is due to the renewal of pre-Christian Nature religions including Wicca, Shamanism, Witchcraft, and Druidry. Modern Pagans are well acquainted with Lady Raglan's idea that the Green Man in churches was a portrayal of their pre-Christian deities, and his image can be seen as saying, "See, I never went away, and now I'm out in the open again."

Yet even without theories as to his historical meaning, the Green Man is a perfect image for Nature-focused spirituality. He cannot be limited to any single religion or philosophy—which makes him a perfect poster boy (poster plant?) for the growing numbers of "spiritual but not religious" believers.

The popular art-and-culture festival called Burning Man, held annually in Nevada, featured the Green Man as its art theme for 2007. The festival site explained:

> Peering outward from behind a mottled screen of vines and leaves, the Green Man does not speak or sleep;

The poster for the 2007 Burning Man festival featured a modern version of the Green Man.

The Perennial Green Man **195**

he waits. . . . This year we will appropriate the Green Man and the primeval spell he casts on our imaginations for a modern purpose. Our theme concerns humanity's relationship to nature. Do we, as conscious beings, exist outside of nature's sway, or does its force impel us and inform the central root of who and what we are?

The Green Man's resurgence in film, art, festivals, and environmental events must be accounted for at a level deeper than words, of things that issue from the greater depths of our subconscious. Carl Jung proposed that certain symbolic characters—the hero, the dragon, the goddess, for example—are universal archetypes proceeding from humanity's collective unconscious. When we see these figures, we are already familiar with them, even if we have not yet heard their stories, because they are in our ancestral blood. Jung suggests such archetypes rise to the surface of human consciousness when they are especially needed.

The Green Man is certainly needed today. In his postmodern, spiritual, and environmental role, the Green Man is a symbol of hope we can claim both as individuals and as a planetary community. He reminds us of the power and potential of green life to rise and heal the terrible mistakes we have committed.

Medieval people, concerned with mortality and the fate of their souls, saw the face of Adam—who symbolizes each one of us—and the Tree of Life growing hope from his tongue. In our time, we cannot escape the brooding fear that our separation from Nature imperils our collective existence. In such a time, we see in the Green

Man a symbol of our destinies intertwined with the natural world.

Contemplating the Green Man as a symbol for our time, allow me to present alongside him another appropriate concept: Pando. Pando is the world's largest single living organism, and one of the oldest. A quaking aspen grove in Utah that grows from a single root and shares identical DNA with all its parts, Pando is over 80,000 years old, occupies 106 acres, and is estimated to weigh collectively 6,600 tons. Appearing to be a forest, yet actually a single organism, Pando tells us, "What seems to be many is actually one."

When we gaze into the face of Nature, who gazes back at us? In the depths of these eyes, we see reflections of something totally other than ourselves—and also something intimately akin to ourselves.

Ilia Delio, scientist and theologian, wrote, "We used to believe that reality was comprised of little separate 'elemental' building blocks, but now we realize that nothing exists in isolation: rather . . . everything exists as one interconnected whole." This is not magical or fantastical thinking; in stating this, Delio is wearing her scientist hat. Another scientist-cum-theologian, Teilhard de Chardin, explained how the universe is held together by "Love Energy." This energy has been named many things—the Prime Mover, the Tao, Spirit, veriditas, the Great Mystery, the Force, and countless others. There is a growing consensus among spiritual masters and scientific theorists that all things are connected by a unitive reality, which works toward awareness, growth, and renewal.

Advances in science are also pushing us back toward the Middle Ages' awareness of a living, conscious reality to be found in the world of Nature. Scientists have found that the vegetative world is not "unconscious" as we supposed but alive in ways we did not suspect. Richard Powers, in his book *Overstory*, summarizes some of these findings:

> *We found that trees could communicate, over the air and through their roots. . . . We found that trees take*

care of each other . . . seeds remember the seasons of their childhood and set buds accordingly . . . trees sense the presence of other nearby life. That a tree learns to save water. That trees feed their young and synchronize their masts and bank resources and warn kin and send out signals to wasps to come and save them from attacks. . . . A forest knows things. They wire themselves

This is "the Trembling Giant," Pando (from the Latin word for "I spread"). A single genetic male clone, he is the most massive organism on Earth. Sadly, scientists also believe that after surviving for thousands upon thousands of years, today he is slowly dying.

The Perennial Green Man

up underground. There are brains down there, ones our own brains aren't shaped to see. Root plasticity, solving problems and making decisions. Fungal synapses. What else do you want to call it? Link enough trees together, and a forest grows aware.

Powers goes on to remind us: "You and the tree in your backyard come from a common ancestor. A billion and a half years ago, the two of you parted ways. But even now, after an immense journey in separate directions, that tree and you still share a quarter of your genes."

In the light of all this, the Green Man speaks to us, communicating both assurance and challenge. His message is for all of us collectively and each of us individually, and it is both ancient and ever-new.

In *Wildwood: A Journey Through Trees*, Roger Deakin writes of the Green Man:

The leaves flow from him like poems or songs. He himself is a kind of folksong. Everyone knows it, but each singer has a different, personal version, a variation on the theme. . . . He is the spirit of the rebirth of nature. He is the chucked pebble that ripples out into every tree ring. He is a green outlaw and he is everywhere.

What is the secret of the Green Man soul? Perhaps simply this:

We are united—you, me, the plants, the Earth, the Divine—we are all one.

Green Men started out primarily in churches, but eventually, they moved out into the world of everyday life, with their first appearance being on pub signs. This image is inspired by the sign for a pub called the Green Man in Soho, London. "Green Man" became a popular pub name during the seventeenth century, and there are still many pubs with that name in the United Kingdom.

Image Credits

Watercolor plant elements

Andrey Yanushkov | Dreamstime.com

Green Man illustrations

Micaela Grace

Chapter 1

Page 14: Rudolf Ernst | Dreamstime.com

Page 15: Kenneth McIntosh

Page 16: Jude Tarrant and the studio team of Sunrise Stained Glass Ltd, www.stainedglassartists.co.uk, 58-60 Middle Street, Southsea, Portsmouth, Hampshire UK.

Page 17: Micaela Grace

Page 20: Kechristensen7 | Dreamstime.com

Chapter 2

Page 26: (from left to right) Dorieo,

Wikimedia Commons; Christ Church Cathedral; Wikimedia Commons

Page 27: (from left to right) Liné 1; Ed Meskens; St. John's Cemetery, Bangor, Pennsylvania

Page 28: (from left to right) Moleskine; Poliphilo; Southwell Minster; Exeter Cathedral; Southwell Minster; Abbaye de la Trinite, Vendome

Page 30: Andy Scott

Page 31: Parish Church of Ottery St. Mary

Page 32: Kenneth McIntosh

Page 34: Kenneth McIntosh

Page 35: Marsha McIntosh

Chapter 3

Page 40: Prosthetic Head

Page 41: Jörg Bittner Unna

Page 42: St. David's Cathedral, Wales

Page 43: St. David's Cathedral, Wales

Page 44: Hereford Cathedral

Page 46: Kenneth McIntosh

Chapter 4

Page 52: Marsha McIntosh

Page 54: DeFacto

Page 55: (from left to right) Kuhwert; Kognos; Steve Cadman; Steve Cadman

Page 56: (from top to bottom) Kenneth McIntosh, Southwell Minster

Page 59: Norwich Cathedral

Chapter 5

Page 62: Christ Church Cathedral, Dublin

Page 64: The Church of St. Mary

Page 65: Rahara Church

Page 67: (from top to bottom) Rodw; Wells Cathedral, Wells Cathedral

Page 75: Gallica Digital Library

Page 76: Jezcolton | Dreamstime.com

Chapter 6

Page 80: Medieval Heritage

Page 81: Medieval Heritage

Page 82: Avebury Henge Shop, https://www.hengeshop.com/products/green-man-oak?variant=46110544468

Page 83: Vic Burton

Chapter 7

Page 89: Staff Sgt. JoAnn Makinano

Page 90: Disdero

Page 91: Eigenes Werk

Page 92: (from left to right) Wikimedia Commons, Corinium Museum

Page 95: Julianna Lees

Page 96: Cambridge University Library

Page 97: public domain

Page 98: public domain

Chapter 8

Page 103: Newell Convers Wyeth (1882–1945)

Page 104: The Cannon Group

Page 105: public domain

Page 106: Robert Thorley | Dreamstime.com

Page 108: Hadrianus 1959

Page 109: Nessy-Pic

Page 110: Tony Grist

Chapter 9

Page 114: Helen Hotson | Dreamstime.com

Page 115: Janeh15 | Dreamstime.com

Page 116: Thomas Smith | Dreamstime.com

Page 117: Carl Potter | Dreamstime.com

Page 118: Micaela Grace

Page 119: Alexerina27000 | Dreamstime.com

Page 120: Kenneth McIntosh

Page 121: public domain

Page 122: Thomas Smith | Dreamstime.com

Page 123: public domain

Page 124: Kenneth McIntosh

Page 125: Kenneth McIntosh

Chapter 10

Page 128: Julie Denham | Dreamstime.com

Page 129: Kenneth McIntosh

Page 130: public domain

Page 132: Edmund George Warren, 1859

Page 133: Quotidian Theatre Company

Chapter 11

Page 139: Andrew Shiva

Page 140: public domain

205

Chapter 12

Page 145: St. Andrew's Church, Bulmer
Page 146: Ellyn Sanna
Page 147: Kenneth McIntosh
Page 150: Kenneth McIntosh
Page 151: Kenneth McIntosh

Chapter 13

Page 156: Poliphilo
Page 157: public domain
Page 159: Kaxjan
Page 161: Poliphilo
Page 162: Amanda Slater
Page 163: British Heritage
Page 164: British Heritage

Chapter 14

Page 168: Funkydiscopops
Page 169: Tim Bekaert
Page 171: John W. Schulze

Chapter 15

Page 177: Kenneth McIntosh
Page 181: public domain

Chapter 16

Page 186: Kenneth McIntosh
Page 187: public domain
Page 188: Lucas Cranach
Page 189: Kenneth McIntosh
Page 192: Kenneth McIntosh
Page 193: Tony Hisgett
Page 194: Susan Vineyard | Dreamstime.com
Page 195: Burning Man Project
Page 197: Ellyn Sanna
Page 199: J. Zapell
Page 200: Stuart Pearcey | Dreamstime.com

Water from an Ancient Well

Celtic Spirituality for Modern Life

A Fresh Look at Celtic Spirituality

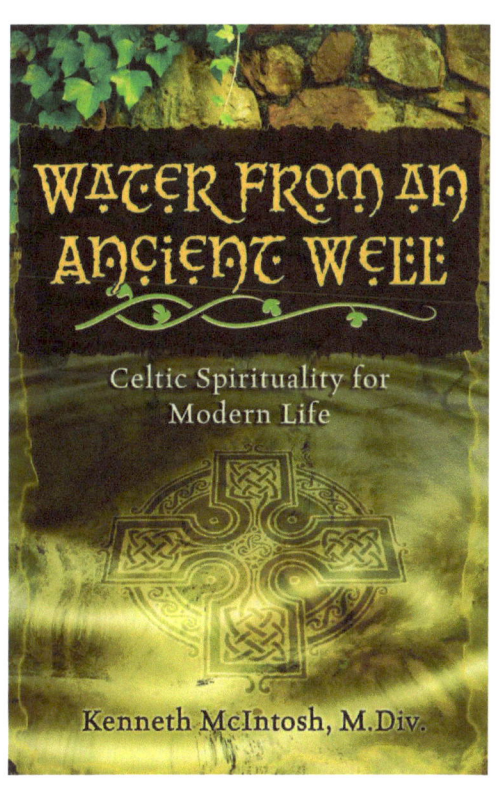

Using story, scripture, reflection, and prayer, this book offers readers a taste of the living water that refreshed the ancient Celts. The author invites readers to imitate the Celtic saints who were aware of God as a living presence in everybody and everything. This ancient perspective gives radical new alternatives to modern faith practices, ones that are both challenging and constructively positive. This is a Christianity big enough to embrace the entire world.

by Kenneth McIntosh

Paperback Price: $19.99

E-book Price: $7.49

Brigid's Mantle

A Celtic Dialogue Between Pagan and Christian

Pagan and Christian Join Hands within Celtic Spirituality

Long ago, the story goes, Brigid flung out her mantle over the world. Beneath its shelter, the Earth and its people could find healing, insight, and growth. This legend, shared by both Celtic Pagans and Celtic Christians, makes the point that a mantle is not a box, a small rigid container meant to keep some things inside while excluding others. Instead, a mantle is wide, flexible, inclusive. Using this as their central metaphor, the authors—one a Pagan healer and the other a Christian minister—engage in a dialogue that is ultimately about what it means to be spiritual, to be a person of faith. While the authors agree that very real differences separate Paganism and Christianity, they affirm that shared points of understanding can be found under "Brigid's Mantle." They build on a concept of Celtic spirituality that embraces the arts, Nature, the supernatural world, compassion for those in need, and gender equality.

by Lily Weichberger & Kenneth McIntosh

Paperback Price: $14.95

E-book Price: $5.99

Celtic Nature Prayers
Prayers from an Ancient Well

Find God in Nature Pray for Our Endangered Planet

Long before they had heard about Christianity, the Celts knew that Nature was their portal to a great spiritual reality. Wells, mountain crags, caves, and lochs were "thin places" that allowed access to the realm of spirits. In these temples of Nature, the Celts sought physical and spiritual healing, as well as revelation. The salmon, the eagle, and even the tiny hazelnut, all were allies in helping humanity access the mysterious magic that underlay physical matter.

by Kenneth McIntosh with Lucie Stone

Paperback Price: $14.95

E-book Price: $5.99

CONTEMPLATIVE COLORING
The Green Man

More and more people are rediscovering what they already knew when they were kids—coloring is fun. What's more, coloring can lead us into a deeper awareness of both our inner selves and the world around us.

The Green Man images in this coloring book have been paired with short quotations from two of Anamchara Books' titles: *The Green Man: Ancient Symbol for the Modern World* and *Celtic Nature Prayers: Prayers from an Ancient Well*, both by Kenneth McIntosh. These quotations are offered for use as mental focal points as you color, with space provided for you to jot down any thoughts that may rise to the surface.

As you color, you may find yourself connecting with Nature in a new way, experiencing what poet Elizabeth Browning described: *"Earth is crammed with heaven and every bush aflame with God."*

Paperback Price: $11.99

CONTEMPLATIVE COLORING
CELTIC BESTIARY

The images in this coloring book were drawn from medieval bestiaries, and the descriptions of the animal are summaries compiled from actual ancient texts. Although today we may no longer believe that a panther's breath is so sweet that it draws everyone to her . . . or that barnacle geese grow on trees . . . or that mermaids even exist, we still can learn from these fantastical bestiary creatures, just as medieval readers did. Each animal included here, from dragons to goats and unicorns to crocodiles, is a delight in its own right. Each one allows us to engage with the Divine as the ancient Celts did—and as we might have when we were children—using our imaginations, our creativity, and our hands to connect mind, heart, and body with God and Creation.

Paperback Price: $11.99

www.ingramcontent.com/pod-product-compliance
Lightning Source LLC
Chambersburg PA
CBHW041601070526
44586CB00003BA/41